The Bedford/St. Martin's
ESL Workbook

The Bedford/St. Martin's ESL Workbook

Sapna Gandhi-Rao
University of Louisville

Maria McCormack
Columbia University

Elizabeth Trelenberg
Florida State University

Bedford/St. Martin's
Boston ■ New York

Manufactured in the United States of America.

0 9 8 7 6
f e d c b a

For information, write: Bedford/St. Martin's, 75 Arlington Street,
Boston, MA 02116   (617-399-4000)

ISBN: 0-312-44503-2

EAN: 978-0-312-44503-4

Contents

To the Instructor

The discussions and exercises in this workbook are designed to provide additional instruction and practice for students who are non-native speakers of English. The 100 exercise sets cover the grammar, punctuation, mechanics, and usage issues that ESL students typically find challenging.

Most of the exercise sets are written as connected discourse with a thematic focus that allows students to read and revise their work in context. You may wish to assign some of these exercises in conjunction with topics covered in class, or you may prefer to have students work on specific difficulties you've identified in their writing. The answers to all exercises are provided in an appendix so that students may check their work independently.

The last exercise in each section is a writing prompt that encourages students to write their own paragraph, applying the grammar covered in that section. These prompts, called "Taking the Next Step," can be assigned as soon as students complete the exercises in each section, while the material studied is still fresh. The workbook's editing guidelines and glossary help students understand editing conventions and unfamiliar terms.

More exercises are available on Exercise Central, the online exercise database at bedfordstmartins.com/exercisecentral, and on the CD-ROM, *Exercise Central to Go: Writing and Grammar Practice for Basic Writers*.

If you would like more information about these materials or about the complete supplements package for your textbook, please contact your local Bedford/St.Martin's sales representative or e-mail sales_support@bfwpub.com.

To the Student

The difference between the formal English you use in your writing and the informal English you use in everyday conversation complicates the already formidable task of learning the English language. In fact, formal English can sometimes seem like a completely different language from conversational English. But just as practice in listening to and speaking English helps your conversational skills, practice in reading and writing English will help your writing skills.

This book was designed to help you master formal written English by providing extensive grammar practice through exercises. The book is organized into parts based on particular grammar areas; the exercises range from basic identification tasks to fill-in-the-blank activities to locating grammatical errors within texts. At the end of each section you will find an exercise entitled "Taking the Next Step." These exercises are intended to keep you thinking about the skills you've practiced and to help you put them to use in your own writing.

Whether you use this book in conjunction with other writing textbooks or use it alone to hone your writing skills, we hope that you become more confident writing in English as you strengthen your abilities.

Part 1
Nouns

A noun is a word that names a person (*sister, fireman*), place (*prairie, supermarket*), thing (*magazine, peanut butter*), or concept (*love, justice*). Proper nouns name specific people, places, things, or concepts (*Andrea, Nevada, Ford Theater, Confucianism*). Collective nouns name groups (*dozen, gang, herd*). Nouns that have both singular and plural forms are called **count nouns**.

Singular and Plural Nouns

Nouns that end in **consonant + *y*** form the plural by replacing the **-*y*** with **-*i*** and adding **-*es***.

Singular	Plural
party	parties
baby	babies
lady	ladies

Some nouns do not follow these rules in forming the plural. It is best to memorize these irregular plural forms as you encounter them.

Singular	Plural	Singular	Plural
man	men	woman	women
child	children	ox	oxen
foot	feet	goose	geese
mouse	mice	louse	lice
fish	fish	sheep	sheep
syllabus	syllabi	stimulus	stimuli
datum	data	speculum	specula

Note that patterns in forming the plural exist even within these irregular plural forms.

Count Nouns

Count nouns are used—as the name indicates—for items that you can count individually. Most count nouns add **-*s*** or **-*es*** to form the plural.

-s		-es	
book	books	watch	watches
car	cars	kiss	kisses
sea	seas	dress	dresses
desk	desks	potato	potatoes
ant	ants	tomato	tomatoes
hand	hands	bus	buses

Noncount Nouns

Noncount nouns are used for items that are difficult or impossible to count, although you may specify quantities indirectly (*two gallons of gas, a liter of blood, five blades of grass, three cubes of ice, a dozen ears of corn*). Below are some commonly used noncount nouns.

Food and drink

bread	cocoa	milk
butter	coffee	pasta
cabbage	corn	rice
candy	flour	salt
cereal	fruit	sugar
cheese	ice	tea
chicken	meat	water

Gases, liquids, and materials

air	gold	plastic
alcohol	helium	rain
blood	iron	steel
gasoline	oxygen	wood

Abstract nouns

advice	freedom	knowledge
anger	happiness	love
beauty	health	poverty
courage	information	truth
		wealth

Other common noncount nouns

clothing	money	weather
furniture	research	work
grass	traffic	

Some nouns can be either count or noncount, depending on their meaning.

Count   As the bride and groom ran out of the chapel, family and friends pelted them with tiny **grains** of rice.

Noncount The draft horses consumed a great amount of **grain** every day.

When learning new nouns in English, you should consult a dictionary or a reliable online source to determine whether a noun is count, noncount, or both.

Exercise 1.1 Singular and Plural Nouns

For each of the following sentences, underline the appropriate singular or plural noun from the pair in parentheses.

> **Example:** The professor gave several (handout/<u>handouts</u>) about immigration to the class.

1. Many (immigrant/immigrants) to the United States at the turn of the twentieth century came from Europe.

2. They crossed hundreds of miles of (ocean/oceans) to escape poverty and political problems.

3. Many immigrants were fleeing from disease, which killed thousands of Europeans in many (country/countries).

4. Immigrants also came from different (corner/corners) of the world to the United States seeking their fortunes.

5. Problems drove some people away from their native countries, but others came to the United States because they wanted to own a few acres of (land/lands) or find opportunities that were unavailable at home.

6. One of the most heavily used (port/ports) of entry for immigrants to the United States was Ellis Island in New York Harbor.

7. When they arrived at Ellis Island, immigrants had to pass a number of (test/tests).

8. Anyone with symptoms of tuberculosis, smallpox, or other contagious (disease/diseases) had to return home on a departing ship.

9. Some immigrants spoke little English, and people from certain cultures were also unfamiliar with the twenty-six (letter/letters) of the alphabet used in the United States.

10. Many immigration (official/officials) at Ellis Island gave these people Americanized names.

Exercise 1.2 Singular and Plural Nouns

Revise each sentence to correct any errors in the use of singular and plural noun forms. Some sentences might not contain any errors.

      Example: The Beatles broke up more than thirty year ago.

1. The Beatles were one of the most popular musical act of all time.

2. Four young man from Liverpool, England, made a fortune playing songs that young people loved.

3. Recordings by the Beatles still sell millions of copy today.

4. Some buyers are middle-aged fans who have not lost respects for the group.

5. They may buy CDs since they no longer own stereo equipment that can play their old vinyl records.

6. Playing musics from their youth makes some fans feel young again.

7. Other people who buy Beatles records are teenager discovering the songs for the first time.

8. Even today, a teenager is likely to know bits of Beatle trivias.

9. Some young listeners become fans, but others don't understand the fusses about the Beatles.

10. The two surviving Beatles are in their early sixties, but their fans span all age.

Exercise 1.3 Singular and Plural Nouns

Using the word in parentheses, fill in the blank with the appropriate singular or plural form.

Example: The group of _____*children*_____ (child) ran into the park.

1. The United States Postal Service is the oldest _____ (agency) of the federal government.

2. It was formally established in 1775 after several _____ (attempt) by private citizens, the British government, and local statesmen to create a system for sending and receiving mail.

3. Benjamin Franklin played a key _____ (role) in making the service efficient and profitable.

4. Postal roads stretched from Maine to Florida, so that _____ (rider) could deliver the mail they were sworn to protect.

5. This security assured American _____ (colonist) that their communications would not be intercepted by the British government.

6. One famous U.S. _____ (president), Abraham Lincoln, also served as postmaster.

7. As the United States grew, so did the number of postal roads and _____ (employee).

8. The Postal Service is part of the federal government and as the _____ (country) grew, so did the power of the Postal Service.

9. Horseback was only one method for delivering the mail; it was also delivered by steamboat and by _____ (train).

10. Since its establishment, the Postal Service has served the American people in _____ (time) of peace and war.

Exercise 1.4 Count and Noncount Nouns

Underline the appropriate noun in each of the following sentences.

> **Example:** Early immigrants to the United States often got bad (<u>information</u>/informations) about their new country.

1. A large (number/amount) of European immigrants moved to the United States by steamboat.

2. The new immigrants had different (reason/reasons) for leaving their homeland to come to this country.

3. Many (immigrant/immigrants) came here seeking new opportunities.

4. Some sought freedom of religion, and some sought (wealth/wealths).

5. (Overpopulation/Overpopulations), famine, and disease also drove people to leave their homeland.

6. In addition, (discrimination/discriminations) by the government and police in some countries spurred emigration.

7. Immigrants to the United States have often faced (battle/battles) with current residents over jobs, housing, and their facility with English.

8. (Legislation/Legislations) to discourage immigration increased in the last decade of the twentieth century.

9. For example, the Immigration Reform Act of 1995 made it clear that immigrants have to become citizens before they can qualify for Social Security (benefit/benefits).

10. Many immigrants today need the (advice/advices) of other immigrants, government officials, and social service agencies to learn what rights they have.

Exercise 1.5 Count and Noncount Nouns

Revise each of the following sentences to correct any errors made with count and noncount nouns.

        Example: Recently, ~~researches~~ ^{research} into American views on love showed that most young ad̂ults were looking for a soul mate.

1. According to a recent survey by the National Marriage Project, many young people in the United States believe that they will find one special person to offer them true loves.

2. The idea that every person has a soul mate can build dangerously high expectation.

3. When people expect perfect romances, they may end relationship that are imperfect.

4. Young adults need to be realistic when they think about the quality they want in a life partner.

5. Many marriage end because the partners have unrealistic ideas about married life.

6. A potential partner's appropriatenesses as a parent did not matter much to most people who took the survey.

7. Only 16 percents of the young adults surveyed believed that the main purpose of marriage is to have children.

8. The idea that a couple should have common beliefs about religions was also viewed as unimportant.

9. Is the United States becoming a nation of young romantic?

10. Perhaps too many young people are getting their informations about marriage from television and romance novels instead of from real-life examples.

Exercise 1.6 Count and Noncount Nouns

Underline the appropriate noun from the pair in parentheses.

Example: Most people look forward to taking long (vacation, <u>vacations</u>).

Hawaii is a chain of (1.) (island, islands) in the Pacific Ocean. The warm (2.) (weather, weathers) brings visitors from all over the world. The abundance of (3.) (fruit, fruits) is also an attraction; there's nothing like eating a fresh (4.) (pineapple, pineapples) for breakfast. Another attraction is the natural beauty of Hawaii's geographical (5.) (feature, features) such as volcanoes, waterfalls, and beaches. Enjoying the natural beauty is a great way to find (6.) (relief, reliefs) from a hectic lifestyle. Hawaii also has many natural (7.) (resource, resources). One of them is (8.) (coffee, coffees). Visitors will also find many spas promoting (9.) (relaxation, relaxations). Certainly, Hawaii has inspired many (10.) (people, peoples) to visit again.

Exercise 1.7 Taking the Next Step with Nouns

Write about your favorite foods and any new foods you've tried recently. What are the ingredients? How are these foods cooked? Where did you eat these foods (at home, at a friend's house, in a restaurant)? Be sure to use singular and plural nouns, count and noncount nouns, and the new vocabulary you learned in this chapter. Refer to the relevant sections of this chapter as you work to help master each concept.

_____

_____

_____

_____

_____

_____

_____

_____

_____

Part 2
Articles

The articles *a/an* and *the* belong to a class of modifiers called **determiners**. This workbook treats articles separately from other determiners because they can pose particular difficulties for non-native speakers of English.

A/An

An is a variant of *a* that occurs directly before a word beginning with a vowel sound (not simply beginning with a vowel—pay attention to the way the word *sounds* rather than how it is *spelled*).

> **a** university   **an** umbrella
> **a** helmet   **an** hour

A/an may precede a noun, adjective, or adverb, but it must modify a noun.

> **a** big blue umbrella
> **an** unusually big umbrella

You should use the indefinite article *a/an* when the reader is not likely to know the identity of the noun being modified. Use *a/an* when introducing a noun for the first time.

> On the first day of class, **a** woman came in and announced that the class would meet in another room.

In this sentence, *a* modifies the noun *woman* because the reader doesn't know who the woman is.

The

You should use the definite article *the* when the identity of a noun is expected to be known or is about to be revealed. In some cases, the noun is named earlier in the sentence. In other cases, the knowledge is inferred. You should also use *the* with the superlative and with ordinal numerals (*the first*, *the sixth*, etc.).

> On the first day of class, a woman came in and announced that the class would meet in another room. **The** woman led all the students in the class to the new location.

The modifies *woman* in the second sentence above, since the writer is referring to the woman previously mentioned in the first sentence.

> **A** boy stepped out of his house and began calling his dog. **The** dog came running down **the** street.

The reader doesn't know the identity of the boy, so the indefinite article *a* is used in the first sentence. Because the first sentence specifies the identity of the dog—*his* dog—the definite article *the* is appropriate in the second sentence. The reader assumes the street is the one in front of the boy's house, so again the definite article *the* is appropriate.

Put **the** milk in **the** refrigerator.

In the example above, the reader can assume that there is only one container of milk and likewise only one refrigerator.

The leaves are turning red early this fall.

The reader can assume that this sentence refers to the leaves on the local trees.

The president visited Karen's town while campaigning.

There is only one president of a country at any given time, so the reader can assume that the president mentioned above is the president of Karen's country.

This is **the** best pie I've ever eaten.

The superlative *best* identifies the noun *pie*.

Zero Article

The term *zero article* indicates that there is no need for an article or a determiner. Zero article occurs only with noncount or plural count forms, and it signifies general categories.

I'm afraid to ride **roller coasters**.
She likes **flowers**. **Roses** are her favorite flower.
Our dog liked to chase **cats**.

Note that you do not use *a/an* and *the* with other determiners such as *his*, *its*, *those*, and so on.

Exercise 2.1 Articles

For each of the following sentences, underline the appropriate article from the words in parentheses. **X** means "no article."

Example: (A/An/<u>The</u>/X) love of two people can transcend cultural differences.

1. (A/An/The/X) marriage that unites people from different cultures can be very difficult.

2. However, it is often (a/an/the/X) easiest way to build a relationship with someone from a different culture.

3. After all, (a/an/the/X) love makes people willing to appreciate new things.

4. But people usually have to overcome several obstacles if they consider marrying (a/an/the/X) person from another culture.

5. In some cultures, people believe that men should have (a/an/the/X) main role in supporting a family.

6. A man from one of these cultures might be unhappy with (a/an/the/X) working wife, especially one who earns more than he does.

7. In certain cultures, (a/an/the/X) wives are even considered the property of their husband's family.

8. (A/An/The/X) woman who would be unable to live happily in a male-dominated household should avoid marrying a man from such a culture who has very traditional views.

9. Some people develop (a/an/the/X) interest in their beloved's culture that is so strong that they are willing to leave their own traditions behind.

10. However, many of the happiest crosscultural marriages are those in which the couple finds (a/an/the/X) appropriate balance between their traditions.

Exercise 2.2 Articles

In each of the following sentences, cross out the italicized article if it is unnecessary or incorrect. If the italicized article is necessary, write **C** above it.

> Example: ~~The~~ M̷any Americans disagree about prayer in public schools.

1. The U.S. Constitution guarantees freedom of *a* religion to all residents of the country.

2. The United States does not have *an* established state religion.

3. Instead, by *the* law, all residents are allowed to worship as they please or to choose not to worship at all.

4. The U.S. Supreme Court declared *the* school prayer unconstitutional about forty years ago.

5. Some Americans are still not certain what *the* members of *the* Court outlawed in their ruling.

6. Students in American public schools are not forbidden to pray silently in class—for example, before *a* test.

7. Student religious organizations can meet before *a* school starts.

8. However, teachers or *the* other authority figures in a school may not legally lead prayers in class or at school functions.

9. The U.S. Constitution does not restrict the practice of *the* personal religious beliefs.

10. But the law does not permit the use of *a* class time in public schools for group expression of *a* particular faith.

Exercise 2.3 Articles

Revise each of the following sentences by adding, deleting, or changing articles wherever necessary.

                 The
Example: ˄ Hispanic population of the United States is growing faster than any other minority group.

1. Politicians in the most states now realize the importance of trying to win the Hispanic vote.

2. Grouping all Hispanics together ignores a fact that Hispanic Americans come from many different countries and cultures.

3. Cultures of Cuba and Mexico are different, just as the cultures of France and Sweden are different.

4. Just as not all Irish Americans agree on political issues, there is not the single issue that guarantees all Hispanics' approval.

5. Some issues may capture an interest of the majority of Hispanic American voters, however.

6. A high percentage of Hispanic residents of the United States believe that the government should provide assistance to a poor.

7. Government help to reduce poverty is usually considered liberal position.

8. However, many Hispanic Americans are in the agreement with conservative political opinions about social issues.

9. In 2001, George W. Bush became a first U.S. president to broadcast a speech in Spanish to appeal to Hispanic American voters.

10. His tactic may or may not have had the effect on Hispanic approval of his positions, for Hispanics in this country also disagree about the politics of speaking Spanish.

Exercise 2.4 Articles

In the sentences below, write **a**, **an**, or **the** in each blank.

> **Example:** I waited in line for _____*an*_____ hour to set up my cell phone plan.

1. Cell phone usage in _____ United States has risen dramatically in the last four years.

2. There was _____ time when it seemed that only business people had mobile phones.

3. Mobile phones of _____ 1980s were bulky, heavy objects.

4. Cell phones of _____ new millennium are slim, sleek, and lightweight.

5. _____ cell phone used to cost hundreds of dollars, but now they are sometimes given away with service plans.

6. _____ few of my friends have given up their land lines in favor of using cell phones for all their calls.

7. There has been _____ drastic increase in usage among teenagers.

8. They believe that cell phones are _____ absolute necessity.

9. After all, maintaining _____ social life is important when you are sixteen years old.

10. The parents of _____ teenager would probably disagree.

Exercise 2.5 Taking the Next Step with Articles

Write about the most exciting thing you've ever done. Where did it happen? Who was with you? Why was it exciting? Be sure to use the articles *a, an,* and *the* and words that use the zero article plus any new vocabulary. Refer to the relevant sections of this chapter as you work to help you master each concept.

_____

_____

_____

_____

_____

_____

_____

_____

_____

Part 3
Pronouns

Pronouns take the place of nouns, other pronouns, or phrases functioning as nouns. You can use them to avoid repetition of previously mentioned words. The word or group of words replaced by the pronoun is called the **antecedent**. Usually pronouns occur after you have already stated the antecedent, although they may also occur before the antecedent. Pronouns must agree with their antecedents in case, number, and gender; therefore, it is important to know their different forms and how they function in a sentence. Before selecting which pronoun you will use, be sure to look at its position and function in the sentence.

Examine the use of pronouns in each of the following examples. The pronoun is in **boldface** type and its antecedent is underlined.

Personal Pronouns

Pronouns that function as the subject of a sentence or clause are called **personal pronouns**. (These are also sometimes called subject pronouns.)

		Singular	Plural
First person		I	we
Second person		you	you
Third person	*masculine*	he	they
	feminine	she	
	neuter	it	

Audrey went to the store for eggs. **She**'ll be back shortly.

The red scarf hung on the coat rack where someone left **it** a long time ago.

Since **he** had been working indoors all afternoon, Nicholas needed some fresh air. (*pronoun precedes the antecedent*)

Colin, can **you** help me open this window? **It**'s stuck.

Leanne and I had planned to watch a movie, but **we** went swimming instead.

Object Pronouns

Pronouns that function as the object of a sentence or clause are called **object pronouns**.

		Singular	Plural
First person		me	us
Second person		you	you
Third person	*masculine*	him	them
	feminine	her	
	neuter	it	

Since <u>Tom</u> was going out in the rain, Cindy gave **him** the large umbrella.

<u>My cousins</u> are in town this week, so I'm going to the museum with **them**.

<u>That mud puddle</u> is deep. Don't step into **it**.

<u>The woman</u> in line at the post office let us go in front of **her**.

Possessive Pronouns

Pronouns in the **possessive case**, also called **possessive pronouns**, are used to show possession or ownership.

		Singular	Plural
First person		my/mine	our/ours
Second person		your/yours	your/yours
Third person	*masculine*	his	their/theirs
	feminine	her/hers	
	neuter	its	

<u>Nicholas</u>, you should buy this tie for **your** father.

The further <u>Julie</u> hiked, the heavier **her** backpack seemed.

<u>Mike</u> has to travel a lot for **his** job.

Our son just learned how to walk.

You should use the possessive pronouns *mine*, *yours* (singular), *hers*, *ours*, *yours* (plural), and *theirs* only after a helping verb. You can use *his* and *its* before a noun as well as after a helping verb.

This house is **hers**.	That's **her** house.
The fault is **mine**.	It's **my** fault.
Which car is **his**?	That's **his** car.
That's **yours**.	That's **your** wallet.

Note that while nouns use **apostrophes** to show possession, pronouns have their own special forms to show possession and do not use apostrophes. A pronoun with an apostrophe is a **contraction**, not a possessive pronoun. It is easy to confuse these forms because they are **homonyms** (words that are pronounced the same but spelled differently). Compare the following possessive pronouns with their homonym contractions.

Possessive pronouns	Contractions
its = belonging to it	it's = it is
your = belonging to you	you're = you are
their = belonging to them	they're = they are

Exercise 3.1 Personal Pronouns

Underline the correct pronoun from the pair in the parentheses.

Example: When our son comes home from school, (he, they) is always happy to
see the dog.

1. (I, She) get great satisfaction from knowing my family eats nutritious food.

2. (They, He) tell me what they like, and I cook what pleases them, as long as it's healthy.

3. (We, You) eat breakfast together on Sundays. It gives us time to talk and be together.

4. Our youngest son is two years old. (He, They) likes mushy oatmeal because he can play
   with it.

5. Susan, our neighbor, sometimes comes over for breakfast. (I, They) am good friends
   with her.

6. (I, They) like to cook a special meal for my husband after he comes home from a long
   business trip.

7. (He, They) is not particular about what he eats. He will eat anything I cook for him.

8. A couple of times a month, (we, she) eat at a nice restaurant; it's a special treat for us.

9. If (we, he) take the kids, it's a very special treat for them too.

10. (I, They) always enjoy cooking at home because it relaxes me.

Exercise 3.2 Personal Pronouns

Circle the correct pronoun from the pair in parentheses.

Example: Lasagna is a delicious Italian pasta dish, but (it, its) gives me heartburn.

1. If (you, he) have a dog, it is a good idea to train it.

2. (You, He) should hire a trainer because your pet will be more responsive to a professional.

3. People are more likely to train dogs than cats. (They, You) believe dogs are easier to train.

4. A trainer teaches dogs to behave around strangers. Otherwise, (they, he) may bark, bite, or attack us.

5. Young children are especially at risk because (they, we) like to pet dogs, but owners want to make sure their dog won't harm them.

6. When (you, she) take your dog for a walk, you will probably put a leash on it.

7. (We, They) take our dogs for long walks, and sometimes they wrap their leashes around us.

8. One of our dogs is female, and (he, I) love taking her on long walks.

9. Both of our dogs let children rub their bellies, and (they, he) love licking the children's faces.

10. (They, She) don't even mind when our cats play with their doggy toys.

Exercise 3.3 Personal Pronouns

Underline the correct pronoun from the pair in parentheses, and write the antecedent above it.

> **Example:** The weatherman predicted twelve inches of snow, but (*weatherman* <u>he</u>, you) has been wrong before.

1. Mahatma Gandhi was a spiritual and political leader of India, and (he, they) was admired and respected by many people.

2. After experiencing discrimination as a lawyer, (we, he) decided it was up to him to change society's laws about discrimination.

3. He married when he was thirteen years old; (they, he) and his wife had grown up together, so he knew her well before they married.

4. When Gandhi had established himself as a leader, (he, we) built an ashram with his wife and family. People from around the world came to live with them.

5. When my father was a young boy, he saw Gandhi at a rally. My father said, "(I, they) think he looked at me."

6. Since (we, they) visited the Gandhi Institute for Nonviolence in Tennessee, sometimes the Institute sends us newsletters.

7. (They, I) enjoyed the visit so much that it made a lasting impression on me.

8. (I, You) had always read books about Gandhi, but I had never known before what motivated him.

9. Gandhi was motivated by a deep spiritual belief, and (he, it) helped many others recognize it.

10. (They, He) believed that love and compassion would conquer the hatred in the world. Do you agree?

Exercise 3.4 Personal Pronouns

For each of the following sentences, fill in the blank with the correct pronoun.

> **Example:** Religion and politics are topics that spark discussion, but
> _____I_____ never discuss them with my co-workers.

1. Francis Scott Key, a lawyer in Georgetown, wrote the national anthem of the United States more than 200 years ago _____ is still sung today.

2. The song inspires many Americans. _____ place their right hands over their hearts when they sing it.

3. The anthem has a challenging melody, so _____ isn't easy to sing.

4. If _____ forget the lyrics, people will often hum along.

5. _____ have the lyrics memorized in our household.

6. _____ get emotional when I hear the anthem; it moves me to tears.

7. When we hear the national anthems of other nations, _____ also mean something to us.

8. When the national anthem is sung before sporting events, _____ is meant as a reminder.

9. A famous female singer performed the anthem at Super Bowl XXXVIII; _____ did a fantastic job and earned a round of applause from the crowd.

10. Francis Scott Key wrote a beautiful anthem, and _____ would be proud to know just how often it is sung.

Exercise 3.5 Personal Pronouns

For each of the following sentences, fill in the blank with the correct pronoun.

> **Example:** _____ We _____ buy bags of candy for our kids every Halloween.

1. You probably know that the United States holds a presidential election every four years. _____ should get to the polls early if you want to avoid long lines.

2. Presidential nominees spend a lot of time and money spreading their message. _____ hope to represent the values and beliefs of American citizens more accurately than the other candidates do.

3. The president of the United States is the most powerful man in the government. _____ is elected by electors in the Electoral College.

4. George Bush is the current president of the United States. _____ was re-elected in 2004.

5. Although there has never been a woman president in the United States, some political analysts say that Senator Hillary Clinton might run for president in 2008. _____ is best known as the wife of former president Bill Clinton, but she is also a powerful politician in her own right.

6. Citizens vote for one nominee over another because _____ feel one candidate will guide the country more effectively than the other one.

7. In many states, _____ can cast your vote by marking a ballot at home and mailing it in.

8. _____ have voted in every election because participating in democracy is important to me.

9. _____ is only one type of government, but many western nations try to convince other countries to choose democracy.

10. Ultimately, people of all nations want the type of government that works best for them; _____ want to live comfortable, happy lives just like anyone else.

Exercise 3.6 Personal Pronouns

Underline the correct pronoun from the pair in the parentheses. Write the antecedent above it.

        receptionist

    Example: The receptionist seems to be helpful, but (they, <u>she</u>) actually hates it when people ask questions.

1. When my cousin told me she was getting married, (we, I) knew exactly what I wanted to give her.

2. (She, He) had always wanted to have her favorite band perform at her wedding. When I found them, I knew it was the perfect gift.

3. The band leader said he would do something special, but (they, he) would not tell us what that special thing would be.

4. When the band surprised us in Halloween costumes, (we, he) didn't know it was them.

5. The drummer wore a Dracula costume, and (he, we) looked good.

6. My cousin was disappointed with the band until (they, he) sang a song just for her.

7. Then (she, we) felt better, and the band's costumes didn't bother her anymore.

8. The band tried to put a costume on the groom, and (he, they) was taken completely by surprise.

9. Luckily, (he, we) is very tall and the costume didn't fit him.

10. The band played dance music the rest of the evening, and then (they, we) thanked us for having them.

Exercise 3.7 Object Pronouns

Underline the correct pronoun from the pair in parentheses.

> **Example:** I like to study at the public library. The librarians there help (<u>me</u>, us) find what I need.

1. The Odyssey is the story of King Odysseus and his travels after the Trojan War. From the beginning of the epic poem, there are powerful forces working against (her, him).

2. Odysseus is twenty years old when he leaves his homeland, the island of Ithaca, and forty years old before he sees (it, them) again.

3. Odysseus is married to Penelope, and he leaves (him, her) behind to raise their son, Telemachus.

4. Penelope believes that Odysseus will come home after the war is over, but she is unaware of the gods' plots to delay (her, him).

5. The war lasts for ten years, and it takes Odysseus another ten years to return to (her, him).

6. During the war, the Greeks fight to bring down the city of Troy, and eventually they do conquer (it, them).

7. Many warriors are killed on both sides, including Achilles, a warrior known for his awful temper. Paris is the one who finally kills (her, him).

8. Odysseus helps win the war with his cunning. The Greeks would not have won (it, them) without him.

9. On his way home, he encounters many situations that delay (him, her).

10. When the weary king finally returns to the people of Ithaca, he is overjoyed to see (them, us).

Exercise 3.8 Object Pronouns

For each of the following sentences, fill in the blank with the correct pronoun.

Example: The power went down in most of the neighborhood, but we didn't lose
_____*it*_____ in our house.

1. While many couples arrange marriages with the partners they choose, sometimes the couples' elders arrange _____ .

2. The woman might even ask her friends to describe _____ for an ad in the local paper.

3. The man's family might send photographs of _____ to the woman's family.

4. The woman's family plays an important role in arranging for eligible bachelors to meet _____ .

5. At the first meeting, the bachelor may talk about his education, family background, or potential for future success. The woman and her family will want to know about all of _____ .

6. If the man and the woman seem suitable for marriage, the parents might arrange _____ right away.

7. If you didn't grow up in a culture with arranged marriages, you might not like having your spouse chosen for _____ .

8. My parents had an arranged marriage, but when I started dating they agreed not to arrange one for _____ .

9. They did not force their views on my sister or _____ ; in fact, they respect our different views of marriage.

10. Both types of marriage can succeed, if the couple remembers their vows and succeeds in honoring _____ .

Exercise 3.9 Object Pronouns

For each of the following sentences, fill in the blank with the correct pronoun.

Example: I bought all the textbooks I needed for my classes, but I got sick the first
day and missed _____them_____ .

1. When I started college, I had no idea how much the college lifestyle would change

   _____ .

2. I went to the state university my first year of college. Then I considered other schools
   and started finding information about _____ .

3. An advantage of attending a state university is that _____ is more affordable than a private university.

4. During my second year, I discovered a state college that seemed more suitable for

   _____ .

5. The folks at the admissions office sent _____ a promotional brochure
   about the school, and I knew _____ was the college for me.

6. After I was accepted, my dad drove _____ to the campus. I was glad to
   have _____ with me.

7. I thought the college campus was beautiful. _____ had green rolling hills
   and towering trees.

8. The first girl I met was also new, and she became my best friend. I helped
   _____ get through the next few years.

9. My father had tears in his eyes as he watched _____ accept my diploma.

10. My graduation happened more than ten years ago, but my father still talks about

    _____ .

Exercise 3.10 Possessive Pronouns

Underline the correct pronoun from the pair in parentheses.

> **Example:** The politician expected to win the race, but even (<u>his</u>, their) own family didn't vote for him.

1. Ray Charles was a pioneer of the music industry who influenced many other musicians with (its, his) music.

2. He was born in Georgia and later moved with (his, her) small family to northern Florida.

3. He and his brother didn't know their father, and Ray's mother raised both of (her, his) sons alone.

4. His mother worked as a laborer to provide as much for (their, her) sons as she could.

5. Ray Charles witnessed his brother's death, and that memory haunted him throughout (his, our) entire life.

6. Ray Charles started losing his vision when he was five years old, but he adjusted to (its, her) absence and continued pursuing (his, her) passion for music.

7. He went to a school for the blind in St. Augustine, where he developed (their, his) technical skills on the piano.

8. He listened to Nat King Cole and Charles Brown, and (his, their) influence is evident in his earlier recordings.

9. He influenced artists in jazz, but many artists in country, gospel, and soul also owe (his, their) success to Ray Charles.

10. He has said that classical music is European but that jazz is (their, our) music, meaning it was born in America and belongs to Americans.

Exercise 3.11 Possessive Pronouns

Circle the correct pronoun from the pair in parentheses.

> **Example:** We always watch the local news to keep up with what's happening in (our, her) neighborhood.

1. Jimmy Carter served as president of the United States from 1977 to 1981, but he is known more for (her, his) peacemaking work after his presidency than for (her, his) domestic work during that time.

2. He and his wife Rosalynn moved to the White House with (their, our) young daughter, Amy.

3. Amy was only ten years old when she left (her, my) hometown of Plains, Georgia.

4. Before becoming president, Jimmy Carter served as the governor of (his, its) state.

5. After his presidency, Jimmy Carter founded the Carter Center, which is guided by (their, his) principles of social justice.

6. Rosalynn Carter helps (my, her) husband manage the Carter Center.

7. In addition to working with him, she devotes time to other of (her, our) favorite causes.

8. The Carters also volunteer for Habitat for Humanity, an organization that helps people build (their, our) own homes.

9. President Carter received the Nobel Peace Prize for (her, his) work promoting peace and economic development throughout the world.

10. President Carter will be remembered in America as one of (its, our) greatest citizens.

Exercise 3.12 Possessive Pronouns

Fill in each blank with the correct possessive pronoun.

Example: He put _____his_____ plate in the dishwasher after lunch.

I first came to the United States when I was five years old to live with

(1.) _____ father. My mother and I left our home in 1973, and it changed

(2.) _____ lives forever. My mother was anxious about leaving

(3.) _____ mother and father and my sister behind. My father missed

(4.) _____ own mother and father at first, but he adjusted to living by himself.

My sister moved to the United States two years later to complete (5.) _____

family reunion.

Initially, I was too shy to talk to (6.) _____ teacher and classmates.

Eventually, I overcame my timid ways and played just like all the other children in

(7.) _____ class.

I have lived in the United States for over twenty-five years, but I still practice some tra-

ditions from (8.) _____ native culture. Most children learn about traditions

from (9.) _____ parents; I learned how to cook from my mother. I only hope

that (10.) _____ own children learn something about our culture from me.

Exercise 3.13 Object/Possessive Pronouns

Circle the correct object or possessive pronoun from the pair in parentheses.

> **Example:** The young physicist doesn't like to share (him, (his)) findings with the other scientists.

1. The American educational system has undergone dramatic change in (it, its) short history.

2. (You, Your) children will most likely receive an education that's very different from your own.

3. Schools used to offer traditional programs for children, but now they provide special programs for (them, their).

4. Some programs ask that children audition, and then accept or reject (their, them) based on (their, them) performance.

5. Some schools offer only one special program, such as drama; if you think your child has an aptitude for (it, its), he or she should apply to a school with that special focus.

6. Some parents believe that a traditional education is best for (their, them) children because the focus is on reading, math, and science.

7. Other parents contend that the traditional programs are too restrictive for (they, their) children.

8. Still other parents only want to be certain that (they, their) children pass state or national achievement tests.

9. Regardless of which program you choose for your children, your involvement demonstrates (your, you) commitment to (their, them).

10. Your children will know that (their, they) education is important to (you, your).

Exercise 3.14 Object/Possessive Pronouns

Underline the correct object or possessive pronoun from the pair in parentheses.

> **Example:** If you return library books late, the librarian will fine (<u>you</u>, your) the next time you borrow books.

1. Golf is a sport that challenges players to perfect (their, them) skills.

2. At the very least, golfers need clubs, golf balls, and gloves to make (their, them) game the best it can be.

3. If I were an amateur golfer, I might take (my, me) clubs to a golf course and hit a few balls to warm up.

4. Professional golfers play for money, so (them, their) equipment is very important to (them, their).

5. Annika Sorenstam plays every hole with great intensity. Her skill impresses (me, my).

6. Tiger Woods is a golfer who executes (his, him) shots with exceptional grace and skill.

7. I enjoy watching a close competition, even if the sport itself bores (me, my).

8. Golf tournaments are often broadcast on television, but they are too boring for (me, my) taste.

9. The most exciting way to experience golf is to watch (it, its) firsthand at a tournament.

10. If you go to a golf tournament, don't forget to bring (you, your) umbrella and sunscreen.

Exercise 3.15 Object/Possessive Pronouns

Fill in each blank with the correct object or possessive pronoun.

Example: We replaced the windows in _____our_____ house because they were damaged in the storm.

1. All parents learn that taking care of _____ children is a full-time responsibility.

2. There are many books about children that advise parents on how to raise _____ .

3. If your son becomes sick, you should tend to _____ illness.

4. If your daughter wants to date, you should meet _____ boyfriend before letting _____ go out with him.

5. Many experts say that parents should be very involved in their children's lives, if they want their children to respect _____ .

6. When we were young children, our parents knew almost everything that happened to _____ .

7. As children grow into teenagers, they share less and less about _____ lives.

8. When I was a teenager, my parents rarely asked _____ to discuss my personal life with _____ .

9. On the other hand, my best friend told _____ parents every detail about her life.

10. Her brother was also very open about _____ personal life; of course, he was only eight years old.

Exercise 3.16 Object/Possessive Pronouns

Fill in the blanks in the paragraphs below with the correct object or possessive pronoun.

Example: The senior managers took their staff out to dinner to show how much the company appreciated _____them_____ .

Doctors are caring people who are genuinely concerned about (1.) _____ patients' health. Some doctors work in hospitals while others have (2.) _____ own practices. Our family doctor is Dr. Tate Rockwell, and I trust (3.) _____ completely. His wife, Marcy, is also a doctor. He helped (4.) _____ set up a private practice a block away, so that she would be working nearby.

My former doctor's office was always busy. Even when his patients didn't have appointments, he never refused to see (5.) _____ . He didn't share his practice with other doctors because they couldn't tolerate (6.) _____ policies. When choosing a physician, you should find a doctor whose philosophy on treatment closely matches (7.) _____ own. This way, you will be satisfied with the health care he provides for (8.) _____ . Otherwise, you could be disappointed with the treatment options offered by (9.) _____ doctor. Good doctors maintain strict schedules because it helps (10.) _____ make sure that (11.) _____ patients receive treatment in a timely manner.

Reflexive and Intensive Pronouns

Reflexive and intensive pronouns have the same forms but function differently. Reflexive pronouns refer back to the subject of the clause in which they occur. Intensive pronouns have the same form as reflexive pronouns and are used to emphasize their antecedent.

First person		myself	ourselves
Second person		yourself	yourself
Third person	*masculine*	himself (<u>never</u> hisself)	themselves
	feminine	herself	
	neuter	itself	

Reflexive pronouns <u>I</u> try not to take **myself** too seriously.

The <u>boss</u> gave **himself** a raise.

<u>You</u> should be good to **yourself**.

Intensive pronouns <u>We</u> installed this carpet **ourselves**.

The <u>professor</u> **herself** acknowledged the student's achievement.

The <u>president of the company</u> **himself** came to the airport to pick up the guests.

Notice that intensive pronouns can be left out of a sentence and the sentence will still make sense, although there will no longer be any emphasis. But removing a reflexive pronoun makes the sentence incomplete.

Intensive	**Correct**	<u>We</u> installed this carpet **ourselves**.
	Correct	We installed this carpet.
Reflexive	**Correct**	<u>You</u> should be good to **yourself**.
	Incorrect	You should be good to.

Be aware that the expression *by + intensive pronoun* or *all by + intensive pronoun* is idiomatic and typically indicates that no other person was involved in the action specified.

We built the shelves **by ourselves**.

Julie made those curtains **all by herself**.

Also, pay attention to the phrase *talking to oneself* and its variants. It is a common expression in English, and it involves a reflexive pronoun.

He assembled the cabinet while **talking to himself** the entire time.

She **told herself** not to make the same mistake again.

He **grumbled to himself** as he wrote a letter of complaint to the manager.

Relative Pronouns

The relative pronouns *who, whom, whose, which,* and *that* link dependent clauses to independent clauses to form complete sentences from two separate ideas. When choosing a relative pronoun, it is important to understand the difference between **restrictive** and **nonrestrictive** clauses. Restrictive clauses contain information crucial to the main idea of the sentence. They cannot be removed without changing the sentence's meaning and they are *not* set off from the rest of the sentence by commas. Nonrestrictive clauses can be left out of a sentence without changing the main idea; they *are* set off from the rest of the sentence by commas.

That/Which

In restrictive clauses, use *that* to refer to animals or things. In nonrestrictive clauses, use *which* to refer to animals or things.

Restrictive clause	The hawk **that was my uncle's pet** was named Tootsie.
Nonrestrictive clause	The hawk, **which had been flying low over the ground**, swooped down to catch a mouse in its talons.
Restrictive clause	The film **that my aunt recommended** turned out to be very entertaining.
Nonrestrictive clause	That film, **which is still showing in the theaters**, is very unusual.

In restrictive and nonrestrictive clauses, use *who, whom,* or *whose* (depending on the function of the pronoun in the dependent clause) to refer to people.

Who

Use *who* when the relative pronoun functions as the subject of the dependent clause.

Restrictive clause	The person **who lives in that brick house** has many kinds of pets.
Nonrestrictive clause	My neighbor, **who lives in that brick house**, adopted a kitten from the animal shelter.

Whom

In formal writing, use *whom* when the relative pronoun functions as the object of the dependent clause. But be aware that in many cases English speakers use *who* or *that* in place of *whom*. When choosing whether to use *whom, who,* or *that*, think about the occasion for writing and who will be reading your writing. *Whom* can sound awkward or pretentious in casual contexts, such as in conversation or e-mail. But *whom* may be a better choice for more formal academic writing. Consult your instructor if you are not sure.

Formal

Restrictive clause	That literature professor **whom everyone knows and loves** is retiring this year.
Nonrestrictive clause	Our professor, **whom the university awarded an honorary degree**, is revered by all.

Informal

Restrictive clause	The customer **who I waited on** was rude.
or	The customer **that I waited on** was rude.
Nonrestrictive clause	The customer, **who we recognized from two days ago**, asked for more coffee.

Whose

Use *whose* when the relative pronoun functions as the possessive pronoun.

Restrictive clause	The man **whose dog ran away** is offering a reward for finding it.
Nonrestrictive clause	My neighbor, **whose dog ran away recently**, is building a fence around his yard.

Exercise 3.17 Reflexive/Intensive Pronouns

Underline the correct pronoun from the pair in parentheses.

> **Example:** The little boy learned how to tie his shoes and dress (<u>himself</u>, herself) for school.

1. If you own your home, there are many projects that you have to do (ourselves, yourself).

2. Some projects are too complicated for homeowners to do (themselves, herself).

3. One way to decide which projects you should do (itself, yourself) is to ask at a hardware or home improvement store.

4. When we asked about adding gutters to our house, the clerk said that he never puts gutters up (himself, themselves).

5. But we thought we would try doing it (yourselves, ourselves) so we could save some money.

6. My wife said she wasn't afraid to climb on the roof (herself, himself) to get the measurements of the roof.

7. Once she gave me the measurements, I went back to the hardware store to buy the materials (myself, ourselves).

8. We started the project on a Saturday morning but quickly realized that we could not finish it (themselves, ourselves).

9. On Saturday afternoon, we called a professional who said he would finish the job (himself, ourselves).

10. Now we have nice gutters, and the only project we do (themselves, ourselves) is gardening.

Exercise 3.18 Reflexive/Intensive Pronouns

Underline the correct pronoun from the pair in parentheses.

Example: He couldn't hang up the large picture by (itself, <u>himself</u>).

1. The woman cut (herself, yourself) while chopping vegetables.

2. Her husband drove her to the hospital (itself, himself).

3. She didn't want to drive (themselves, herself), so she was glad that he volunteered.

4. At the hospital, they sat by (themselves, ourselves) until the nurse took them to see the doctor.

5. The doctor was a young man who worked by (himself, herself) in the evenings.

6. He asked the woman, "How did you hurt (himself, yourself)?"

7. She said, "I'm usually careful with a knife. I've never done this to (myself, herself) before."

8. He said the cut wasn't bad and would require only a few stitches. He did the stitching (yourself, himself).

9. He asked if they needed a ride home, but the couple replied, "We drove here (themselves, ourselves)."

10. The doctor wished them well and said, "I hope you both will take good care of (yourselves, themselves)."

Exercise 3.19 Reflexive/Intensive Pronouns

Circle the correct pronoun from the pair in parentheses.

Example: I watered the garden (myself, ourselves) all summer long.

1. This is a beautiful love story about two people who found (themselves, yourselves) alone one summer.

2. He decided to ask her out (herself, himself), even though he was shy.

3. She didn't let (himself, herself) love him at first.

4. Once they found (ourselves, themselves) in love, they spent all their time together.

5. Then one day she said, "I'm leaving for college, but I don't want to live by (myself, yourself)."

6. He said he couldn't make a life for (herself, himself) while she was in college.

7. He said, "We shouldn't do this to (ourselves, themselves). The separation will be too difficult."

8. But her mother approved of the separation. She said, "This is the best thing you could do for (itself, yourself)."

9. After several years of separation, the girl found (herself, himself) thinking about him again.

10. When she saw him again, he said, "I have been thinking of you (ourselves, myself). I have missed you a lot." She promised not to leave without him again.

Exercise 3.20 Reflexive/Intensive Pronouns

Circle the correct pronoun from the pair in parentheses.

   Example: The baby learned to walk all by (himself) themselves).

1. People who live together have to live by rules. They make up the rules (themselves, itself).

2. In college, I had several roommates, but I always wanted to live by (ourselves, myself).

3. My first roommate was a girl who didn't like to do anything (herself, himself).

4. Our one rule was that we were to always clean up after (ourselves, themselves).

5. My second roommate situation was with two girls and one guy. Until I moved in, they lived by (ourselves, themselves) in a big house.

6. The guy liked to cook for (herself, himself); the rest of us didn't know how to cook.

7. One girl worked at a bank to put (himself, herself) through college.

8. My last living situation was the best: I finally got to live by (myself, itself).

9. When living alone, one has only (oneself, myself) to blame if things are not right.

10. Still, I enjoyed living alone; I only had to make rules for (herself, myself).

Exercise 3.21 Reflexive/Intensive Pronouns

Underline the correct pronoun from the pair in parentheses.

Example: My mother told me she cooked the entire meal by (itself, <u>herself</u>).

1. When Sarah was in college, she was unhappy with the student government. She thought, "If I want things to be better, I will have to do something about it (himself, myself)."

2. She decided to run for student president (herself, itself).

3. She recruited several friends to campaign for her around campus; they even put the posters up (yourselves, themselves).

4. Although her friends helped put up the posters, Sarah knew she had to write her campaign speech (herself, myself).

5. One of her opponents was a fellow named John; he told her (herself, himself) that she would make a good president.

6. Sarah's speech slogan was, "If we want to make our lives better, we have to do it (yourselves, ourselves)."

7. After listening to all the speeches, students decided for (ourselves, themselves) which candidate would best represent them.

8. The voting took place on Thursday afternoon; Sarah voted for (herself, myself).

9. Mr. Smith, the president of the college, counted the votes (itself, himself).

10. On Friday, it was announced that Sarah had won the election. She said, "I'm so happy, I don't know what to say for (myself, herself)."

Exercise 3.22 Reflexive/Intensive Pronouns

Underline the correct pronoun from the pair in parentheses.

>   **Example:** I love sunsets, so I taught (<u>myself</u>, herself) how to take beautiful photo-
>   graphs of them.

1. Sam, the father, decided to build the bookshelves (herself, himself).

2. Sam and Anna picked out the design (themselves, ourselves).

3. One feature of the apartment was a mirror in which you could see (itself, yourself) as
   soon as you entered the room.

4. Anna, the mother, painted each shelf (himself, herself).

5. We went to visit them to see the bookshelf unit (ourselves, themselves).

6. I nearly scared (itself, myself) when I walked into the room because I didn't realize
   there was a mirror at the entrance.

7. Anna (himself, herself) jumped when she saw me jump.

8. The children were organizing their books (themselves, ourselves) on the beautiful
   bookshelf that took up an entire wall.

9. Sam was proud that he had constructed the bookshelf (oneself, himself).

10. We were inspired, too. We went home and started planning to build a bookshelf unit
    (yourselves, ourselves).

Exercise 3.23 Relative Pronouns

Fill in the blank with the correct relative pronoun.

      Example: If you are going to exercise, it is best to pick an exercise
          <u> that </u> you enjoy.

1. Charlie wanted to have a party for all of his friends, but he wasn't sure
   _____ to invite.

2. He asked his girlfriend, Lisa, about the guest list, but she just said, "You should invite
   the friends _____ you like."

3. He picked Saturday night because it was a night _____ would work for his
   friends.

4. Charlie also wanted to have the party in the backyard _____ was so beautiful when the weather was good.

5. A few days before the party he started to plan the menu, _____ consisted
   of simple but tasty appetizers.

6. He realized that most people would come hungry, so he decided to provide food
   _____ would satisfy them.

7. He had also thought of a theme for the party, _____ he kept secret until
   the day of the party.

8. He bought drinks and paper supplies, _____ all matched his theme.

9. After all the guests _____ had been invited arrived, Charlie revealed the
   theme of the party: a marriage proposal.

10. The guest for _____ he had planned the party was pleasantly surprised
    when he asked her to marry him.

Exercise 3.24 Relative Pronouns

Fill in the blank with the correct relative pronoun.

> **Example:** When there is a shoe sale, I have a hard time deciding
> _____which_____ pair of shoes to buy.

1. When Jake decided to buy a car, he didn't know _____ one to buy.

2. He also didn't know _____ to take with him to the dealership.

3. Jake did know _____ he wanted a car that was both affordable and stylish.

4. Jake and his friend, Tom, went to the car dealership _____ came the most highly recommended.

5. All of the salespeople seemed nice, but Jake and Tom still didn't know _____ they trusted most.

6. The first car Jake saw was a compact car _____ was exactly the right size, but he also thought it looked rather plain.

7. The next car, _____ was the most expensive, was roomier and had a sun roof.

8. But the car _____ Jake really wanted was a small sports car.

9. The saleswoman said, "If I know _____ the car is for, I can make a better recommendation."

10. Finally, Jake found the one _____ was right for him, a used sports car with a sun roof.

Name _____ Section _____ Date _____

Exercise 3.25 Relative Pronouns

Combine the two sentences by using a relative pronoun. Underline the relative pronoun. Be sure to add a comma before any nonrestrictive clauses, where necessary.

     Example: I am moving to a small city, that It has only one college.

1. The Taj Mahal is a monument. It is considered one of the most beautiful sites in the world.

2. The Taj Mahal is a memorial. King Shah Jahan built it for his queen, Mumtaz Mahal.

3. It is also an ancient mausoleum. It holds the tomb of Mumtaz Mahal.

4. King Shah Jahan wanted to show his deep love for Mumtaz Mahal. She died during childbirth.

5. The King decreed that the Taj Mahal be built in a special location. It had to be both scenic and close to his palace.

6. The King wanted to build a monument. No one would ever forget it.

7. Shah Jahan selected skilled architects and masons. They came from all over India and the Middle East.

8. The Taj Mahal is made of marble, precious stones, and gems. These materials made it a very expensive project.

9. Every year the Taj Mahal attracts millions of visitors. They are always surprised at the grandeur and size of the monument.

10. The Taj Mahal is an extraordinary monument. It is a testimony to the deep love Shah Jahan had for his wife.

Exercise 3.26 Taking the Next Step with Pronouns

Write about yourself and your family members—their jobs, interests, personalities, pets, hobbies, and so on. Refer to the relevant sections of this chapter as you work to help you master each concept. Be sure to use pronouns carefully and to use new vocabulary in your writing.

_____

_____

_____

_____

_____

_____

_____

_____

_____

_____

Part 4
Negative Statements and Questions

Negative Statements

There are several guidelines to follow in forming negative statements.

1. Add the adverb *not*.

2. Add a helping verb before *not* if one is not already present in the original sentence. If a helping verb is present, it should be placed immediately in front of *not*. (See p. 89 for a definition of helping verbs.)

3. If a helping verb must be added, change the main verb to the base form.

> John is leaving for New York tomorrow morning.
> John is **not** leaving for New York tomorrow morning.
>
> John will take the 6:40 A.M. flight.
> John will **not** take the 6:40 A.M. flight.
>
> John likes to fly.
> John does **not** like to fly.
>
> John checked his luggage at the gate.
> John did **not** check his luggage at the gate.

Questions

Yes/No Questions

Simple yes/no questions, often called **closed questions**, are questions that you can answer with just a yes or a no (or their equivalent).

Follow the steps below to form yes/no questions from declarative sentences that already contain a helping verb:

1. Switch the position of the subject and the helping verb so that the helping verb comes first in the sentence.

2. Replace the period with a question mark.

> He is tired and hungry.
> **Is** he tired and hungry?
>
> We are staying in a motel tonight.
> **Are** we staying in a motel tonight?
>
> They were upset.
> **Were** they upset?

Follow the steps below to form yes/no questions from declarative sentences that do not contain a helping verb:

1. Add the verb *do* in the appropriate tense in front of the subject, making sure it agrees with the subject.

2. Change the main verb to its base form.

3. Replace the period with a question mark.

> I said I would go.
> **Did** I **say** I would go**?**
>
> She starts her new job on Monday.
> **Does** she **start** her new job on Monday**?**
>
> We know our team's score.
> **Do** we **know** our team's score**?**

Open Questions

In English, if information other than yes or no is desired, question words are used. Sometimes they are called the **wh- words**: *who, whom, what, which, whose, where, when, why, how*. The kinds of questions formed with question words are often called **open questions**. As with yes/no questions, they usually require a helping verb. However, the question word must come before the helping verb.

> He went to the dentist yesterday.   **Who** went to the dentist yesterday?
>   **Where** did he go yesterday?
>   **Why** did he go to the dentist?
>   **How** did he go to the dentist?
>   **When** did he go to the dentist?
>   **Which** dentist did he go to? (informal)
>   To **which** dentist did he go? (formal)
>   **What** time did he go to the dentist?

In many cases, you can make an open question from a yes/no question simply by adding the appropriate question word in front of the question.

Declarative sentence	You took the bus.
Yes/no question	**Did** you **take** the bus?
Open questions	**When** did you take the bus?
	Where did you take the bus?
	Why did you take the bus?

In the questions below, notice that when the question word asks about the subject of the sentence, there is no need for a helping verb. When the question asks about the object of a sentence, you must change the word order and use a form of *do*.

Subject questions

Who took my pencil?

Whose dog bit my brother?

Which car won the race?

What kind of mammal lays eggs?

Object questions

What did you take?

Whom did the dog bite? (formal)

Who did the dog bite? (informal)

Which race did the car win?

What do baby mammals eat?

Using the wh- words, we can create the following questions from the sentence below.

Rich quickly ran to the convenience store on the corner this morning to buy cough medicine for his sister Leslie.

Question	Answer
Who ran to the store?	**Rich** ran to the store.
What did he buy?	He bought **medicine**.
What kind of medicine?	He bought **cough** medicine.
Why did he go to the store?	He went **to buy cough medicine**.
When did he go to the store?	He went **this morning**.
How did he run to the store?	He ran **quickly**.
Where was the store?	The store was **on the corner**.
For **whom** did he buy the medicine?	He bought the medicine **for his sister Leslie**.
or Who did he buy the medicine for?	He bought the medicine **for his sister Leslie**.
Whose sister is Leslie?	She is **Rich's** sister.
To **which** store did he run?	He ran to the **convenience** store.
or Which store did he run to?	**or** He ran to the store **on the corner**.

Exercise 4.1 Negative Statements

Form negative statements from the regular sentences by changing the verb.

Example: She ~~dropped~~ the plates when the lights went out.
did not drop

1. In my first year of college, most of my friends chose to study one of the romance languages.

2. More recently, languages such as Chinese or Japanese have been more popular.

3. Studying a new language in the early morning has been satisfying.

4. I learned several thousand kanji characters.

5. Learning the kanji characters also helped me learn Japanese.

6. The Japanese language uses kanji characters in its written language.

7. I practiced speaking Chinese with native speakers at my college.

8. They said that they understood me.

9. I believed they were telling me the truth.

10. I loved learning and speaking another language.

Exercise 4.2 Negative Statements

Form negative statements from the regular sentences by changing the verb.

                    did not have

Example: We ~~had~~ to put shutters on our windows because of the storm.

1. Political scandals have filled U.S. history in the past thirty years.

2. Politicians have been caught stealing, lying, and cheating.

3. President Richard Nixon left the presidential office after the Watergate scandal.

4. Many political scandals have "-gate" in their name because of Watergate.

5. Some politicians have been accused of being involved with crime groups.

6. Sometimes, the public demands resignation.

7. The politician might admit his wrongdoing.

8. Other times, politicians defend themselves against accusations.

9. Some politicians confess publicly.

10. Because of scandals, the public finds it difficult to trust politicians.

Exercise 4.3 Negative Statements

Form negative statements from the regular sentences by changing the verb.

                      did not watch

        Example: They ~~watched~~ movies all afternoon.

1. Before the invention of the modern airplane, people traveled by car or railway.

2. People owned only one car for road trips.

3. Better highways were constructed as more and more people traveled by car.

4. The railway provided an alternate mode of traveling.

5. Railway trains offered luxury accommodations such as sleeping cabins and fine restaurants.

6. People also found a way to travel overseas: luxury cruise ships.

7. Cruise ship operators took into account the length of the journey in their plans.

8. Airlines also began offering luxury accommodations such as first class seats and hot meals on flights.

9. Some airlines even have fully reclining seats and televisions for each passenger.

10. Perhaps one day there will be gyms on airplanes!

Exercise 4.4 Negative Statements

Form negative statements from the regular sentences by changing the verb.

                   did not drink

        Example: He ~~drank~~ eight glasses of water every day.

1. Van Gogh learned to paint as a young man.

2. His paintings can be seen in museums around the world.

3. He is best known for his textured brush strokes.

4. He painted with oil paints to produce rich scenes of nature.

5. Van Gogh was close to his brother, Theo.

6. He suffered from depression and an addiction to absinthe, a strong herbal liqueur.

7. Those two afflictions made his paintings more intense.

8. He died just around the time his artwork was becoming famous.

9. Many collectors and museums have bought his paintings.

10. Van Gogh's famous painting of sunflowers sold for millions of dollars.

Exercise 4.5 Questions

Change the following sentences into yes/no questions.

Example: The Grand Canyon is located in Arizona.

Answer: Where is the Grand Canyon located?

1. The Beatles were from Liverpool, England.

   _____

2. There were four musicians in the band.

   _____

3. Paul McCartney and John Lennon wrote many of the songs.

   _____

4. The band's first successful single was "Love Me Do."

   _____

5. The term for the crazed obsession with the Beatles is "Beatlemania."

   _____

6. The band performed on the *Ed Sullivan Show* in the United States in February 1964.

   _____

7. They also starred in the movie *A Hard Day's Night*.

   _____

8. John Lennon's wife's name was Yoko Ono.

   _____

9. The band's last performance was in San Francisco.

   _____

10. The band officially broke up in 1970.

   _____

Exercise 4.6 Questions

Change the following sentences into yes/no questions.

> **Example:** The annual furniture sale happens every July.
> **Answer:** _Does the annual furniture sale happen every July?_

1. My cousin graduated from law school on Saturday.

   _____

2. His area of concentration is business law.

   _____

3. His undergraduate degree was in history.

   _____

4. He chose history because it seemed like a good pre-law degree.

   _____

5. There were 150 students who graduated with him.

   _____

6. The law school is located in southern Florida.

   _____

7. He plans to take the bar exam in July.

   _____

8. He would like to move to Washington, D.C.

   _____

9. He plans to move with his best friend.

   _____

10. He wants to live in Washington, D.C., because it has so many opportunities.

   _____

Exercise 4.7 Questions

Read each statement, and form a question that would be answered by the statement.

Example: The president threw the first pitch.

Answer: Who threw the first pitch? or What did the president throw?
_____

1. The summer Olympics takes place every four years.

_____

2. It features sporting events such as swimming, running, weightlifting, and gymnastics.

_____

3. Athletes who represent their countries compete for gold, silver, or bronze medals.

_____

4. The summer Olympics of 2004 took place in Greece.

_____

5. The first modern Olympic Games took place in 1892.

_____

6. The decathlon consists of ten events including the hurdles, the high jump, the discus throw, and the pole vault.

_____

7. The marathon, a main event of the Olympics, is a 26-mile race.

_____

8. The United States boycotted the Olympics in 1980 because of a political conflict with the former Soviet Union.

_____

9. The Soviet Union boycotted the Olympics in 1984 because the United States boycotted in 1980.

_____

10. The Olympic flag is made up of five rings to represent the five continents.

_____

Exercise 4.8 Questions

Read each statement, and form a question that would be answered by the statement.

Example: The first player chosen was Tony.

Answer: _Who was the first player chosen?_ _____

1. The motion picture industry has an awards ceremony called the Academy Awards.

   _____

2. The awards ceremony was created to recognize artists who had done exceptional work in the past year.

   _____

3. The ceremony takes place in Los Angeles, California.

   _____

4. The awards ceremony usually takes place in the spring.

   _____

5. Millions of viewers around the world see the ceremony on TV.

   _____

6. Celebrities wear beautiful gowns and tuxedos to the ceremony.

   _____

7. The most popular categories are best picture, best director, best actor, and best actress.

   _____

8. _The Lord of the Rings_ won ten awards in 2004.

   _____

9. Jamie Foxx won the award for best actor in 2005.

   _____

10. The 78th Academy Awards will take place in March 2006.

   _____

Exercise 4.9 Taking the Next Step with Negative Statements and Questions

Write about your least favorite thing to do—and why you dislike it. Or imagine that you've traveled to a foreign country you've always wanted to visit, and that you are interviewing a citizen of that country. Be sure to use negative statements and questions—including yes/no and open questions. Refer to the relevant sections of this chapter as you work to help you master each concept.

_____

_____

_____

_____

_____

_____

_____

_____

_____

Part 5
Sentences and Clauses

Sentence Subjects

In English, the most basic sentences (called **simple sentences**) require a subject and a verb. While in some informal writing and speech you may occasionally omit the subject, in most cases English requires you to state the subject. (Remember that imperative sentences have an implicit *you* as subject: [*You*] Return these books to the library.) Even when no true subject exists, English requires a "dummy" or "empty" subject to fill the subject position. *There* and *it* are commonly used as dummy subjects.

> **There** is enough food for everyone.
> **It** is cold out today.

You must also explicitly state the objects of sentences, even when they are understood.

> He threw the dog **a bone**.
> (not just *He threw*—even if the direct object *bone* and indirect object *dog* are obvious)

> Susan wants **that dress**.
> (not just *wants* or *Susan wants*—even if *Susan* and *dress* are clear from the context of the situation)

Word Order in Sentences

Be careful not to move subjects, verbs, or objects out of their normal positions in English sentences. English usually requires **subject-verb-object** word order. While there is some freedom regarding placement of adverbs, in general you should not separate the verb and its object.

> **Correct**   We **bought a large pizza** for dinner.
> **Incorrect**   We **bought** for dinner **a large pizza**.

Be aware that you may find instances of inverted word order in older English writing or poetry.

Exercise 5.1 Sentence Subjects

For each of the following sentences, underline the appropriate subject from the choices in parentheses. **X** means "no subject necessary."

> **Example:** (It/<u>There</u>/X) is much difference of opinion in the United States about the effects of television on young viewers.

1. Television (it/there/X) is available to almost everyone in the United States.

2. (It/There/X) is almost impossible to avoid television in some public places.

3. Some people believe that (it/there/X) is important for television programs to be constructive.

4. In particular, they argue that (it/there/X) is essential for children to receive positive messages from television.

5. (It/There/X) is much popular support for the idea that violent television shows can harm young viewers.

6. However, (it/there/X) is also true that many adults enjoy violent or graphic programs.

7. Many Americans believe that the media (it/there/X) is not to blame for how we use the information it presents.

8. (It/There/X) are ways for individuals to use media information wisely, many people say.

9. Many Americans argue that (it/there/X) is up to parents or guardians to make sure that children do not watch inappropriate television shows.

10. Most Americans seem to feel that (it/there/X) should not be government censorship of television programs.

Exercise 5.2 Word Order in Sentences

Revise each of the following sentences so that the verb is in the appropriate position.

Example: Most Americans ~~government censorship~~ don't want.

1. Many people that too much sex and violence is shown on television believe.

2. Would like most parents to monitor their children's television viewing.

3. For many people, however, keeping track of a child's choice of television programs impossible is.

4. One solution might from recent technological innovations come.

5. Several years ago, agreed American television manufacturers to start equipping all new televisions with a V-chip.

6. The V for "violence" stands.

7. The V-chip out screens shows that contain sex and violence.

8. Parents the chip program to block shows with certain ratings.

9. With the V-chip, censor individuals, not the government, their children's television programs.

10. Of course, today, many children better than their parents know how to program electronic devices.

Exercise 5.3 Word Order in Sentences

Revise each of the following sentences so that subjects, verbs, and objects are in the correct English word order.

Example: Are there several problems with the V-chip system.

1. The television industry ratings for television programs provides so that parents can decide what to allow their children to watch.

2. The ratings system similar is to the one used for movies.

3. The ratings system exists already, but people get a V-chip only when they a new television buy.

4. Older children might to programming rated as explicit be attracted.

5. Most parents know that want kids what they are not allowed to have.

6. Parents with an older television shows rated for mature audiences will not be able to block out.

7. Say some critics that it is only a matter of time before a child learns to tamper with the V-chip programmer.

8. Advertisers worry that parents will block out the prime-time shows that the most advertising revenue generate.

9. If a show an explicit rating has, parents might block it out and advertisers might shy away.

10. The television industry argues that the V-chip a kind of censorship is since it will indirectly control the kinds of shows produced.

Clauses

A clause is a group of words containing a subject and a verb. Some clauses are **dependent clauses**, meaning that they cannot stand alone as a sentence; other clauses are **independent clauses**, because they can function independently as a sentence in their own right. Dependent clauses are often independent clauses that have a **subordinating conjunction** attached to them.

┌──────── Dependent Clause ────────┐

Subordinating conjunction	+	Independent clause
Although		we left early
Because		we didn't know
If		we had known
When		we arrived at the movie theater
As		we walked into the dark theater
Since		no one was sitting in the front row
Before		the film was over
Until		the end of the movie

Adding an independent clause to a dependent clause creates a complex sentence.

┌──────── Complex Sentence ────────┐

Dependent clause	+ Independent clause
Although we left early,	we were still late for the film because of traffic.
Because we didn't know any other routes,	we had to take the congested freeway.
If we had known how bad the traffic was,	we would have left earlier.
When we arrived at the movie theater,	the movie had already started.
As we walked into the dark theater,	I tripped over a popcorn box.
Since no one was sitting in the front row,	we took those seats.
Before the film was over,	I had to use the restroom.
Until the end of the movie,	we didn't notice that our next-door neighbors were sitting behind us.

Compound sentences contain two independent clauses joined by a **coordinating conjunction**. They can be created from two separate sentences.

We were late. We missed the first ten minutes of the film.

We were late **and** we missed the first ten minutes of the film.

Compound-complex sentences have characteristics of both compound and complex sentences.

Although we left early, we were still late for the film **and** we missed the first ten minutes.

Noun Clauses

Noun clauses are clauses that function as nouns within a sentence. You can use noun clauses to combine two sentences into one, with one sentence functioning as the independent clause and the other as the dependent clause embedded within the main sentence. Consider the following sentences.

A When I was packing for a camping trip, my mother suggested **B**.

B I should bring a small first-aid kit.

C When I was packing for a camping trip, my mother suggested **that** I bring a small first-aid kit.

Sentence C, a sentence created by combining sentences A and B, shows sentence B functioning as a noun clause within sentence A. More specifically, sentence B has become the object of the verb *suggested*. This noun clause is introduced by the subordinating conjunction *that*. The present subjunctive tense (*bring*) shows that it is not a fact (the first-aid kit has not been brought yet), but a suggestion.

Other subordinating conjunctions you might use to introduce a noun clause are: *when, why, how, although, because, whenever, whether, whichever*, etc.

In some cases, a noun clause can function as the subject of the sentence, but usually the dummy subject *it* replaces a potentially lengthy subject. In the sentences below, sentences D and E are combined to produce sentences F and G. In sentence F, sentence E acts as the subject once we add the word *that*.

D **E** didn't matter to my mother.

E We were just camping out in our backyard.

F **That** we were just camping out in our backyard didn't matter to my mother.

However, it is less cumbersome to move sentence E to the end and use the dummy subject *it*, as shown in sentence G.

G **It** didn't matter to my mother that we were just camping out in our backyard.

Adjective Clauses

Adjective clauses are often used in English to modify a noun; but unlike other modifiers, they come after the noun. They may or may not include a relative pronoun such as *that, which*, or *who*.

The film **he was talking about** was unfamiliar to me.

The book **that had been sitting on the table** now has coffee stains on the cover.

Rita was the only person **who knew why the policy had been changed**.

Each sentence above contains two separate ideas and can form two individual sentences. *The film he was talking about was unfamiliar to me* can produce sentences A and B below.

A He was talking about a film.

B The film was unfamiliar to me.

Sentence A contains the adjective clause; sentence B is the main idea. When these sentences are combined, the subject (*the film*) appears only once. The pronoun *that* may or may not appear in this case without changing the meaning of the sentence.

The film **that** he was talking about was unfamiliar to me.

The film he was talking about was unfamiliar to me.

Note that when the relative pronoun is the subject of a verb in the adjective clause, it cannot be omitted.

The movie critics **who** watched the film gave it positive reviews.

Exercise 5.4 Noun Clauses

Underline the noun clause in each of the following sentences, and identify it as a subject or object clause in the sentence.

> **Example:** U.S. companies in the global economy feel <u>that they must send an increasing number of executives abroad</u>. *object clause*

1. Many companies sending executives abroad believe that their most difficult challenge will be helping their employees deal with culture shock in a foreign environment.

2. How companies can help executives to cope when they return is an even more serious problem.

3. Recent research proves that these professionals are unsatisfied with the way their companies are handling their repatriation.

4. A study reveals that 25 percent of returning employees leave their companies within a year.

5. Whatever investment the company made in the employee is lost when the employee leaves.

6. That so much money is at stake motivates top managers to investigate the reasons for employee dissatisfaction.

7. Many people wonder whether much employee dissatisfaction stems from poor planning by the company.

8. Many returning executives complain that their companies didn't tell them exactly what they would be working on when they returned.

9. A majority of returnees are unable to use the experience they gained abroad, which demonstrates that companies are not thinking ahead.

10. How companies will address these repatriation issues is a challenge for today's business world.

Exercise 5.5 Noun Clauses

Revise each of the following sentences by moving the noun clause to the end of the sentence and, if necessary, adding a dummy subject.

Example: That airlines limit the amount of carry-on baggage has always frustrated business travelers.

Answer: It has always frustrated business travelers that airlines limit the amount of carry-on baggage.

1. Why passengers can only bring two pieces of luggage into the airplane cabin is rarely discussed by the airline industry.

   _____

   _____

2. That these two pieces not exceed certain size requirements is mandatory.

   _____

   _____

3. That travelers couldn't fit everything they needed for a business trip into these small bags was often the case.

   _____

   _____

4. Whichever bags exceeded size restrictions had to be handed over by travelers as checked luggage.

   _____

   _____

5. That the airlines often lost checked baggage irritated many passengers.

   _____

   _____

6. In addition, that checked bags take a long time to arrive at the baggage claim often interferes with busy business travelers' schedules.

   _____

   _____

7. That the airlines have been looking for solutions to this problem is encouraging.

   _____

   _____

8. That airplanes should increase the amount of space available in overhead bins so that passengers can bring more and larger carry-ons has been suggested by major airlines.

_____

_____

9. That airplanes can achieve departure six to eight minutes faster with the larger bins has been shown by recent studies.

_____

_____

10. Whether flight attendants will be happy about this change is uncertain.

_____

_____

Exercise 5.6 Noun Clauses

Revise each of the following sentences to correct any errors made with noun clauses.

Example: That their computer systems are crashing companies would like to discover the reason.

Answer: <u>Companies would like to discover the reason that their computer systems are</u> <u>crashing.</u>

1. Is evident why some companies are becoming concerned about what their employees are doing.

   _____

   _____

2. The amount of e-mail that employees send and receive each day systems administrators can use software to see.

   _____

   _____

3. Is necessary for the company to know that an employee e-mails jokes from a business computer?

   _____

   _____

4. Could be considered a breach of privacy when managers read employees' e-mail.

   _____

   _____

5. One employee said that would sue her company for breach of privacy.

   _____

   _____

6. The systems administrator tells employees that is his job to prevent problems.

   _____

   _____

7. That cause managers to install monitoring software there are many reasons.

   _____

   _____

8. Is true that companies have to buy more bandwidth if their employees send huge amounts of e-mail.

_____

_____

9. Whenever their e-mail is scrutinized but senior executives' e-mail is not lower-level employees are concerned.

_____

_____

10. Is important that managers create an atmosphere that makes employees feel trusted and fairly treated.

_____

_____

Exercise 5.7 Adjective Clauses

Combine each pair of sentences into a single sentence containing an adjective clause.

Example: Teenagers are getting plastic surgery. The number of them is rising.

Answer: <u>The number of teenagers who are getting plastic surgery is rising.</u>

1. I spoke to a surgeon. He said that plastic surgery is sometimes a parent's idea rather than a teen's.

   _____

   _____

2. However, more often the teenager is the one. He or she convinces the parent to pay for procedures.

   _____

   _____

3. High school can be a harsh environment. The slightest physical imperfections can provoke torment and teasing.

   _____

   _____

4. Media images of young men and women show impossibly perfect faces and bodies. Teens are frequently exposed to these images.

   _____

   _____

5. Like it or not, we are living in a superficial culture. Attractive people get better treatment than unattractive people.

   _____

   _____

6. Therefore, people are requesting plastic surgery. Their bodies aren't even fully developed.

   _____

   _____

7. One woman was insistent about changing her appearance. She went to a plastic surgeon's office.

   _____

   _____

8. She demanded to have the wrinkles removed. The wrinkles were around her eyes.

_____

_____

9. There were just two problems. The surgeon pointed out these problems to her.

_____

_____

10. The problems were that she was nineteen years old and that she had no wrinkles. The problems prevented her from having the surgery.

_____

_____

Exercise 5.8 Adjective Clauses

Revise the following paragraph to correct the errors in adjective clauses. Some sentences may contain no errors.

> **Example:** For people ~~which~~ ^{who} are considering plastic surgery, there is a new way to prepare for the procedure.

   Nowadays, there are several Internet sites that they show live broadcasts of cosmetic surgery. If people miss the live coverage, they can pull up archival video footage in that patients undergo procedures from liposuction to facelifts. This new trend shows that plastic surgery has gone from something was considered shameful or vain to something is considered normal or even a status symbol. The ten million Americans who had plastic surgery in the 1990s represent every social stratum. Moreover, the majority of Americans whose had plastic surgery came from households that they earned below $60,000. The popularity of the Web casts also demonstrates how much people love to watch live procedures which there is a lot of blood and gore. How do patients feel about being the subject of broadcasts in that their bodies are sliced open? Apparently, just fine; the procedures, are free for patients who model for Web casts, attract hundreds of e-mails per day from candidates.

Mood and Conditional Sentences

Mood

The term **mood** refers to how the speaker intends a statement to be understood: as a fact (the **indicative** mood), as a command (the **imperative** mood), or as a desire, suggestion, or improbability (the **subjunctive** mood). Most kinds of speaking and writing use the indicative mood. You may also have used the imperative mood when giving instructions or directions, such as "Please shut the door" or "Go down the street and take a left at the light." However, subjunctive sentences occur less frequently and may require more attention on your part to use them properly. Consider the following sentences in the subjunctive mood:

Desire	The customer insisted that her money **be** refunded.
Suggestion	My adviser urged that I **take** my prerequisites before my electives.
Improbability	If I **were** an astronaut, I would take my dog with me into space.

The form of the verb determines the mood of a sentence. Present subjunctive is the base form of the verb (the infinitive without *to*). Past subjunctive is the same as the simple past for all verbs except *be*. The past subjunctive of *be* is always *were*. (See Verbs on p. 85 for a review of tenses.)

Conditional Sentences

Conditional sentences are complex sentences that often use the subjunctive mood. You can create them by combining a dependent clause (usually beginning with *if*) with an independent clause. (See Clauses on p. 68.) In spoken or written English, conditional sentences express action-and-result relationships: if one thing happens, then another thing results. *If* is usually explicit; *then* is often understood and therefore is usually omitted. In these kinds of sentences, English also distinguishes the degree to which the speaker or writer believes something to be true. In the examples that follow, observe how the indicative and the subjunctive verb forms indicate the speaker's/writer's belief in the likelihood of the statement.

When the speaker/writer believes the ***if* clause** is likely to happen, the indicative (not the subjunctive) is used. (Remember, the indicative expresses facts, while the subjunctive expresses improbabilities and impossibilities.) The statement below makes a generalization and does not refer to a specific time, so the present tense is used.

If you **get** enough sleep at night, you **function** better during the day.

In the next sentence, the speaker/writer makes a prediction about the future rather than a simple generalization. In this case, the present indicative must be used in the *if* clause and the future indicative in the **then clause** to state the consequences of an action that the speaker/writer believes is likely to happen.

If you **get** enough sleep at night, you **will function** better during the day.

When the speaker/writer doubts that the *if* statement will be acted upon, the past subjunctive is used in the *if* clause and *would* + the base form is used in the *then* clause.

If you **got** enough sleep at night, you **would function** better during the day.

Another alternative to the past subjunctive in this case is *were* + the infinitive, as in the following sentence.

If you **were to get** enough sleep at night, you **would function** better during the day.

When the speaker/writer states an impossibility in the present or in the future, the past subjunctive is used in the *if* clause and *would* + the base form is used in the *then* clause.

If you **slept** with your eyes open, you **would see** how well you sleep.

In the example below, both the *if* statement and the *then* statement have occurred in the past: the chance to get enough sleep in order to function better on that particular day no longer exists.

If you **had gotten** enough sleep at night, you **would have functioned** better during the day.

The speaker/writer is implying that there was too little sleep and, consequently, poor performance. It is possible to express this idea more directly (and therefore a bit less politely) without using a conditional sentence, as in the example below.

You didn't get enough sleep last night, so you didn't function well.

Exercise 5.9 Conditional Sentences

For each of the following sentences, underline the appropriate verb form from the pair in parentheses.

Example: If an instructor asks that her students (are/<u>be</u>) prepared to discuss a book for class, should they be allowed to watch a "book-to-movie" adaptation prior to the class discussion?

1. Some instructors say that if students (had/will have) access to film versions of the reading assignments, they would neglect to do the reading.

2. An instructor may insist that students (not watch/will not watch) a film version if the class has not yet discussed of the reading material.

3. If another instructor (is/were) asked, he might say that watching the film, when done in conjunction with the assigned reading, would enhance the students' learning experience.

4. Such instructors maintain that if students (are/were) to watch only the film version, the quality of their comments would reveal that they had not read the book.

5. Even if students watched a film version of an assigned book, seeing the film by no means (would take/will take) the place of reading the book.

6. Also, students may feel that their learning experiences are being limited if they (are/were) not permitted to watch the film version.

7. Some educators are afraid that if a film adaptation of every book (is/were) to exist, students would quit reading books altogether.

8. If students (turn/had turned) to visual media instead of reading their assigned texts, educators feel that the importance of reading will be minimized.

9. A few instructors may even feel that if completion of reading assignments (isn't/wasn't) enforced, film as a medium will supplant literary texts.

10. If film (had become/becomes) the preferred medium for the transmission of ideas, will books become obsolete?

Exercise 5.10 Conditional Sentences

In the following paragraphs, fill in the blanks with the appropriate form of the verb in parentheses. You may use modals. More than one answer may be correct.

Example: If people really (want) _____wanted_____ to protect their privacy, they would be less willing to give information to stores and Web sites.

If a company (1.) (want) _____ personal information about its customers badly enough to pay for it, should customers give up their privacy for discounts? A drugstore chain in my neighborhood has begun to offer a discount card; if customers have this card, they (2.) (receive) _____ substantial discounts on purchases. The discounts (3.) (appear) _____ when the card is swiped if the customer has purchased selected products. However, customers have to submit personal data such as name, address, salary, age, and telephone number if they (4.) (want) _____ to receive the discount card.

When a clerk at the store asked me if I (5.) (want) _____ to sign up for a discount card, I said no. I thought that if I provided the store with personal data, they probably (6.) (sell) _____ it to a marketing firm, and then I (7.) (start) _____ to receive a lot of junk mail and telemarketing calls. The clerk said that the information would not be sold, but if I (8.) (believe) _____ that, I wouldn't have refused the card. After all, if the company (9.) (not plan) _____ to sell this information, why are store clerks collecting it?

A friend told me that she (10.) (fill out) _____ a form for the discount card if she shopped at that store. "They (11.) (use) _____ information about your favorite products to target you as a customer if you sign up," she said. "Why not let them do that if you (12.) (be) _____ already a customer of the store?"

If I change my mind about the discount card, I (13.) (think) _____ about filling out the form with false information. Even if I (14.) (be) _____ homeless, my friend told me, the store would value my business. "All people who shop there should be eligible for the discounts, even if they (15.) (not have) _____ a home

address and telephone number," she said. I (16.) (end up) _____ visiting the

drugstore as Jane Doe if I decide that my friend is right.

Exercise 5.11 Taking the Next Step with Sentences and Clauses

Write about an event (a play, a concert, a homework session, etc.) you recently attended with your friends. Describe the event. How did you get there? What did you do? How did you get home? Be sure to use sentence subjects, noun clauses, and adjective clauses carefully, and pay attention to word order, mood, and conditional tenses. Refer to the relevant sections of this chapter as you work to help you master each concept.

_____

_____

_____

_____

_____

_____

_____

_____

_____

Part 6
Verbs

Verbs are words that show action or states of being. You use them to join the subject to the rest of the sentence. All complete sentences contain at least one verb, which should be in agreement (singular or plural) with the subject of the sentence.

Tenses

A verb tense is the form a verb takes to show when something took place. All verbs except for the verb *to be* have five forms. *To be* has three present-tense forms and two past-tense forms.

Base form	Present (*-s form*)	Present participle	Past tense	Past participle
work	works	working	worked	worked
file	files	filing	filed	filed
watch	watches	watching	watched	watched
be	am/is/are	being	was/were	been

You can form the **infinitive** by adding *to* to the base form: *to work*. (See Appendix B for a full conjugation of the verb *work*.) The base form and infinitive are not interchangeable, so be sure to avoid substituting one for the other.

You have probably noticed that English has many irregular verbs whose past tense and past participle forms often differ. Consult a dictionary to determine whether or not a verb is irregular.

Simple Tenses

Use the **present tense** to show actions that take place in the present or to show repeated or habitual actions. To form the present tense, use the base form with all subjects except for the third person singular. To form the third person singular, add *-s* to the base form.

He **likes** football.

I **work** on Tuesday evenings.

This machine **operates** efficiently.

Jack and Mary **paint** their house a different color every year.

The **past tense** shows actions that occurred at a particular time in the past. Often a specific time is stated in the sentence. To form the past tense, add *-ed*, *-d*, or *-t* to the base form.

They **worked** for that company a long time ago.

We **vacationed** in Hawaii last October.

The sudden noise **startled** me.

He **slept** well last night.

The **future tense** states an action that will take place in the future. To form the future tense, add *will* to the base form of the verb.

Jose **will work** on that leaky faucet this afternoon.

Her mother **will ask** her to babysit this weekend.

They **will finish** the project by next week.

I'll go by train or bus.

The expression *be going* followed by the infinitive can also be used in a future sense, particularly to state a plan or intent to be carried out in the future.

We **are going to fix** the air conditioning before it gets hot.

Wendy and Dan **are going to visit** Boston in the fall.

I'm going to get my driver's license as soon as I turn sixteen.

She**'s going to look** for a job in the summer to pay for her tuition.

Progressive Tenses

The **progressive** or **continuous tenses**, as they are sometimes called, focus on action in progress or continuing action. You can form them by adding *be* in the appropriate tense to the present participle (*-ing*) form of the main verb.

The **present progressive tense** conveys an action in progress (rather than a completed act). It shows what is happening now. The present progressive tense is formed with *be* in the present tense plus the present participle form.

He **is working** on a solution to that problem.

The dogs **are howling** so loudly that I can't hear myself think.

Dongmei **is sewing** a dress for her daughter.

The **past progressive tense** shows an ongoing action or state in the past that was in progress for a while but is now no longer taking place. Often this tense shows an action in progress interrupted by or taking place at the same time as another action. You can form the past progressive with the past tense of *be* plus the present participle form.

He **was pacing** up and down the room in agitation.

Sharon **was babysitting** when a salesman came to the door.

We **were watching** TV when the electricity went out.

The **future progressive tense** shows action that will begin at a point in the future and will be ongoing for a specified or unspecified period of time. It is formed with *will* + *be* plus the present participle form.

A world-famous soprano **will be singing** at our local opera house.

The boys **will be shooting** baskets after school.

I **will be going** for a walk soon.

Perfect Tenses

While the progressive tenses convey continuous actions or ongoing events, the **perfect tenses** usually convey facts or completed events. You can form present and past perfect tenses by adding the appropriate form of *have* to the past participle form (not the past tense) of the main verb. You can form the future perfect by adding *will have* to the past participle form.

The **present perfect tense** shows an action that occurred or began at a particular point in the past and is still ongoing in the present or has some bearing or effect on the present. It is formed with *have* in the present tense plus the past participle of the main verb.

We **have lived** in Texas for eight years now.

Yasushi and Aiko **have e-mailed** us several times.

Her husband **has rebuilt** their computer's hard drive.

The **past perfect tense** shows an action that occurred in the past before another event in the past. It may be helpful to think of this form as a "super-past" or "double-past" form: it's as far in the past as you can get in English with a single verb form. The past perfect is often used with another verb in the simple past tense (see the underlined verbs in the examples below). It is formed with the past tense of *have* plus the past participle of the main verb.

I **had gone** to college for two years before I <u>chose</u> a major.

Lap **had worked** as a tour guide in Vietnam for three years before he <u>earned</u> enough money to buy a motorbike.

Kim **had managed** to do the dishes, vacuum the floors, and wash the windows before her guests <u>arrived</u>.

The **future perfect tense** shows an action that has begun in the present, is currently ongoing, and will end at a certain time in the future. It is formed by adding *will* + *have* to the past participle form of the main verb for all persons, numbers, and genders.

By the time we get home, we **will have driven** over 2,000 miles in our car in a month.

In May I **will have earned** my degree.

Next summer Tom **will have finished** his book.

The **present perfect progressive tense** indicates an ongoing or continuous action begun in the past and continuing into the present. It is sometimes used with another verb in the simple past tense. You can form the present perfect progressive by using *have* in the appropriate tense plus *been* plus the present participle of the main verb.

I **have been waiting** for this moment for a long time.

Teho and SoYoung **have been looking** for a house for several months.

Juanita **has been taking** piano lessons since she <u>was</u> old enough to sit at the piano bench.

The **past perfect progressive tense** conveys an action that was ongoing for a period of time in the past but is now no longer occurring. Usually this tense shows one action interrupting another action. The past perfect progressive is formed by using *had* + *been* plus the present participle of the main verb.

The ice skater **had been performing** flawlessly when she suddenly fell.

It **had been raining** for days when at last the clouds broke.

Stocks **had been climbing** rapidly when the market fell.

The **future perfect progressive tense** shows an action that has begun in the present and is ongoing into the future, at least up until a time usually named in the sentence. It is used to make projections. You can form the future perfect progressive with *will* + *have* + *been* plus the present participle of the main verb.

> In November, Lucas **will have been working** on his dissertation for two years.
>
> At the end of the marathon, the participants **will have been running** for thirty miles.
>
> Olivia **will have been studying** Japanese for four years at the end of this semester.

Active and Passive Voice

When referring to verbs, the term **voice** indicates whether the subject is acting (**active voice**) or being acted upon (**passive voice**). The tenses in the previous examples are in active voice, because they show the subjects' actions. You should use the passive voice when the acting agent is unknown or not of great importance in the context of the sentence. You can also use it to hide the agency responsible for the action. To form the passive voice, use *be* in the desired tense followed by the past participle form.

> The diamond necklace **was stolen**.
>
> Russian **is written** in the Cyrillic alphabet.
>
> Someone **has eaten** the last piece of pie.

Modals

Modals are auxiliary verbs used most often in making requests and giving instructions. They must be followed by the base form of the verb. The nine most commonly used modals are the pairs *can/could*, *will/would*, *shall/should*, *may/might*, and *must* (which has no pair). In some cases the second modal in the pair refers to the past.

> Elise **can** read a 200-page novel in three hours.
>
> Monica **could** read when she <u>was</u> four years old.

But in most cases, modals usually refer to the present or future. To refer to the past, you must use the modal followed by a perfect auxiliary.

> If you **have** any questions, you **should go** to the instructor.
>
> If you **had** any questions, you **should have gone** to the instructor.

Note that *must* uses *had to* for its past tense.

> We **must** get that contract notarized by 5 P.M. today.
>
> We **had to** get that contract notarized by 5 P.M. yesterday.

When making requests, using the past form of the modal pairs does not change the tense, but instead causes the request to sound more polite because it is less direct. Using different modals can also change the force of a request.

More Direct			More Polite

←——————————————————————————————→

Will you get me a drink?

             Can you get me a drink?

                         Would you get me a drink?

                                    Could you get me a drink?

Here *will* is the most direct; *can* is less direct, *would* is even more polite, and *could* is the mildest form.

Modals can also convey your feelings regarding the certainty of a statement.

Uncertain   **Certain**

←──→

It **might** be time to go by now.

It **may** be time to go by now.

It **must** be time to go by now.

Forming Verb Phrases

You can construct verb phrases from a main verb and one or more auxiliary verbs (also called **helping verbs**) such as *be, have, do,* and the modals *can/could, will/would, shall/should, may/might,* and *must.* When forming verb phrases, keep in mind the following rules.

- Verbs must agree with the subject. Sometimes the subject can be challenging to locate when it is separated from the verb by a prepositional phrase or an adjective clause, or when the subject is a compound subject.

- Verbs must indicate the time of the action in the sentence by using the past, present, or future tenses. Paying attention to expressions of time in sentences can help you choose the correct tense.

- Except when forming questions, auxiliary verbs require a specific word order: *modal + perfect have + progressive be + passive be.* (See "Questions" on p. 49 for more information.)

- Only one modal verb should be used in a verb phrase and it must be followed by a base form. (See Modals on p. 88.)

- The base form is never used after any form of *be.*

Exercise 6.1 Simple Present Tense

For each of the following sentences, circle the appropriate verb from the pair in parentheses.

> **Example:** Mobile Bay (plays, playing) host to one of nature's most unusual phe-
> nomena.

1. A cry of "Jubilee!" (means, meant) that a multitude of fish and crabs have come ashore in Mobile Bay.

2. No one (knew, knows) for sure what causes a jubilee to happen.

3. Some people believe that a lack of oxygen in the water causes the fish and crabs to (swim, swam) closer to the shore and surface.

4. When a jubilee (occurs, occurred), people grab nets and buckets to easily collect an abundance of sea life.

5. Jubilees always (happened, happen) in the summer, often just before dawn.

6. Local citizens (wished, wish) that they could predict when a jubilee will take place.

7. Some locals (believe, believed) that they can predict a jubilee by watching the weather.

8. Calm water in the bay the day before, a gentle wind blowing from the east, a rising tide, and overcast sky, some believe, (foretell, foretold) a jubilee.

9. Yet jubilees sometimes (took, take) place without all of these conditions present.

10. Regardless of what causes a jubilee, the citizens of the Mobile Bay area (thank, thanks) Mother Nature for the delicious gift.

Exercise 6.2 Simple Past Tense

Write the past tense form of the verb in parentheses in the blank.

> **Example:** The whale (dive) _____*dove*_____ deep into the ocean to search for krill.

1. The waves (crash) _____ against the side of the schooner as the captain reconsidered the validity of his voyage.

2. He (think) _____ that he knew the exact location of his daughter, but now he was not certain.

3. Pirates (capture) _____ her three days ago from her home on Serendipity Island.

4. The rogues of the pirate crew (dare) _____ her father, Captain Westbrook, to come find her.

5. The pirates (leave) _____ a note demanding a lofty ransom for the safe return of his daughter, Genevieve.

6. Captain Westbrook (know) _____ that his daughter was tough, but he wanted to find her as soon as possible.

7. The first mate of Captain Westbrook's crew (come) _____ to the worried father to tell him that his crew supported him 100 percent.

8. When Captain Westbrook and his crew (reach) _____ the shore of Broken Bone Cove, he knew his hunch was right.

9. The first mate (find) _____ Genevieve sleeping in an open tent, and she was rescued.

10. What a surprise for the pirates the next morning when they (discover) _____ that she was missing, and on her pillow was a note from Captain Westbrook daring the pirates to come find him.

Exercise 6.3 Present and Past Tenses

For each of the following sentences, circle the appropriate verb from the pair in parentheses.

> **Example:** When I first came to the United States, I (can/~~could~~) speak only a few words of English.

1. When I came to this country, I (go/went) to a huge school.

2. I (remember/remembered) that my fourth-grade teachers used to give me books of pictures and alphabet letters.

3. Before long, however, I (become/became) very good at reading.

4. When my family made me return to my native country, I (am/was) so depressed that I didn't leave the house for weeks.

5. They told me, "You (have to/had to) go to school."

6. Three years later, history (repeats/repeated) itself, and my family returned to the United States.

7. I told my American friends that I (am/was) glad to be back.

8. Two years later, I (graduate/graduated) from high school with a 3.87 GPA.

9. The following fall, I (start/started) college.

10. Now I (take/took) courses in business and computer programming to prepare for a career.

Exercise 6.4 Present and Past Tenses

In each of the following sentences, change the italicized verb to the appropriate tense.

> **Example:** Several years ago, many states _began_ administering standardized tests in
> public schools.

1. In 1995, my eighth-grade teacher told us we *have* to take our state's math and reading tests at the end of the school year.

2. My teacher *spends* the whole spring of 1996 drilling us on the practice tests.

3. School officials came to our class and announced that students *cannot* pass or fail the test.

4. Instead, they said that our school and the teachers *are* being tested.

5. The students agreed that nobody *is* fooled by the officials' remarks.

6. My friend Hector said, "The test results *were* going to be sent to our parents."

7. In May of that year, we *sit* in class every day for a week completing the test.

8. I *score* in the fiftieth percentile, so my results were exactly average.

9. Now I think of those results and *remembered* the eighth grade fondly.

10. I still believe that kids *learned* more in school when less time is spent on test preparation.

Exercise 6.5 Perfect Tenses

Fill in the blank with the correct perfect verb tense. Then identify each verb as present perfect, past perfect, or future perfect tense.

Example: Alex ___has taken___ (take) his final exam in chemistry. *present perfect*

1. Our university student body president _____ (consider) running for public office upon graduation.

2. Upon graduation, she _____ (spend) four years serving the students of Farris University.

3. Before college, she _____ (serve) in high school student government.

4. By her first day after graduation, Megan _____ (provide) a total of eight years in student government.

5. Her parents _____ (hope) that Megan would attend medical school to become a pediatrician.

6. Megan _____ (try) to persuade her parents to embrace her potential career choice in the area of public service.

7. They consistently remind her that from the time Megan was ten years old, she _____ (dream) of becoming a doctor.

8. Mr. and Mrs. Wilcox _____ (want) Megan to make a difference in the world through practicing medicine.

9. Megan _____ (assure) her parents that no matter what she chooses, she will work diligently to make the world a better place.

10. By the time of commencement, Megan _____ (decide) on a career choice, and she is planning to announce what it is during her address to the student body.

Exercise 6.6 Progressive Tenses

Of the two choices in parentheses, underline the choice that is correct.

Example: Jason (<u>will be accepting</u>, will accepted) a position with a Web design company.

1. The Alford family (are moving, is moving) to Austin, Texas.

2. Dr. Alford (was teaching, is teaching) at the University of Texas during the past three summers, and he has hoped that he would one day teach full-time.

3. Dr. Alford (was receiving, was received) wonderful evaluations from his students.

4. The chancellor (were noticing, was noticing) how respected he was, and so the chancellor offered Dr. Alford a permanent teaching position.

5. His family (be hoping, is hoping) that they will enjoy living in Austin for the entire year.

6. They (was visiting, were visiting) during the summers when Dr. Alford taught, and they always enjoyed their visits.

7. Dr. and Mrs. Alford (are hunting, is hunting) for a house in Austin today.

8. They (will looking, will be looking) for a home that is near the university campus.

9. The children (are wishing, is wishing) for a house near the park.

10. No matter where they live, the Alford family (is looking, are looking) forward to Dr. Alford's dream being realized.

Exercise 6.7 Modals

For each of the following sentences, underline the appropriate modal from the pair in parentheses.

Example: Fifty years ago, most people (cannot/<u>could not</u>) learn to use computers.

1. Today, few Americans (will/would) consider living without the conveniences they take for granted.

2. People in the United States (can/could) perform many daily tasks easily because tools to simplify life are widely available.

3. Financial tasks are one example of chores that (will/would) have been more difficult in the years before home computers.

4. Now, Americans (can/could) use computers to view their accounts and pay their bills.

5. With the right computer software, ordinary people (may/might) do their own taxes rather than hire accountants or try to understand the fine print in tax forms themselves.

6. Software today includes more information about current tax law than most people know, and software of all types (should/would) continue to become more sophisticated.

7. Household chores (can/could) also take more time if Americans did not have appliances made more efficient by technology.

8. What modern kitchen (will/would) be complete without an automatic dishwasher?

9. Washing dishes by hand (would/should) take more human effort than loading a dishwasher, and filling a sink to wash dishes (might/may) even use more water than running the machine.

10. (Would/Will) Americans ever miss doing chores the old-fashioned way?

Exercise 6.8 Modals

Revise each of the following sentences to show the correct use of modals.

Example: Before I enrolled at the university, I thought that getting any kind of
degree ~~will~~ _would_ help me get a job.

1. I soon discovered that I must choose a major after two years of coursework.

2. I cannot decide what career field interested me most, so selecting a major was difficult.

3. At the beginning of my third year of coursework, I must make a choice.

4. My adviser told me that I can change my mind later if I decided I wasn't happy with my decision.

5. I decided that I will study engineering.

6. When I took my first engineering course, I discovered that I can't understand some of the math required to complete my homework assignments.

7. I realized that I would have taken more advanced math courses to prepare for my engineering classes.

8. Now I am taking an extra math course to catch up, and I would finish my engineering degree next spring.

9. I can't wait until I start work as an engineer.

10. In the meantime, my professors tell me that I would study diligently to prepare for my career.

Exercise 6.9 Modals

For each of the following sentences, fill in the blank with an appropriate modal and the correct form of the verb given in parentheses. More than one answer may be correct.

> **Example:** People who are considering travel outside their native country
> ___should learn___ (learn) about the culture and language of the country
> they plan to visit.

1. If I had planned the time before my trip more carefully, I _____ (study) the language and culture before traveling.

2. In my first few weeks out of my own country, I _____ (struggle) to communicate in all my interactions with people.

3. I _____ (consider) returning to my native country immediately, but I knew I would regret it later.

4. If I hadn't been so curious about the country I was visiting, I _____ (stay) in my apartment.

5. But, in order to make the most of my time away from home, I knew I _____ (venture) out on my own and face the language barrier.

6. Now, after living here for more than a year, I _____ (enjoy) the culture much more, because I have learned the language well.

7. In fact, I _____ (have) a difficult time readjusting to my native environment if I returned.

8. If I returned home now, I am afraid that I _____ (feel) the same alienation in my native country that I felt when I first arrived in this country.

9. Besides, I _____ (miss) my new friends if I left this country.

10. When my family comes to visit me here, I _____ (prepare) them for the many cultural differences I encountered here over a year ago.

Exercise 6.10 *To be* Verbs

For each of the following sentences, underline the appropriate form of the verb given in parentheses.

> **Example:** The Benny Goodman Orchestra (<u>was</u>, were) famous for playing big band music.

1. Attending orchestral concerts (is, are) a great source of fun for people of all ages.

2. Matt, Ling, and I (are, am) attending a concert tonight.

3. It (is, be) a big band concert featuring the works of Benny Goodman, complete with dancing.

4. Big band music (were, was) extremely popular in the 1930s and 1940s, packing dance halls across the nation.

5. When big band music played, couples (was, were) filling the dance floor with swing dancing.

6. Matt and Ling (are, am) hoping that a swing dancing contest will be held at the concert tonight.

7. They (was, were) practicing their swing dance moves last night until midnight.

8. They (is, are) leaving soon so that they can claim a seat with a good view of the stage.

9. I (am, are) meeting them at the venue at six o'clock.

10. I wonder if you know how to swing dance, because I (are, am) going to learn and I need a partner.

Exercise 6.11 *To be* Verbs

Fill in the blank with the correct form of the *to be* verb.

Example: At this moment, Laura _____is_____ in line waiting to buy tickets.

In the past, Neal (1.) _____ quite a frivolous spender. He and his friends

(2.) _____ frequently investing most of their paychecks in dining out and

entertainment. His parents cautioned Neal that he (3.) _____ squandering his

money and that he needed to (4.) _____ more conscientious about his spend-

ing. Neal realized that his parents (5.) _____ right. He worked diligently to

develop a budget for himself. This strategy worked, and in fact Neal (6.) _____

now very frugal. He packs a lunch to take with him to work, and he (7.) _____

now a regular at the dollar movie theater. I (8.) _____ impressed with the

changes that he has made. Though Neal once (9.) _____ a person who was a

free spender, he (10.) _____ now a person with a hefty balance in his savings

account.

Exercise 6.12 Verb Phrases

For each of the following sentences, underline the appropriate verb form from the pair in parentheses.

> **Example:** In California, hundreds of millions of dollars (spent/<u>are spent</u>) annually to provide bilingual education to students with limited proficiency in English.

1. Bilingual education programs are (regard/regarded) as a failure by many Americans.

2. Many graduates of these programs have not (learn/learned) good English skills.

3. The United States would (face/facing) a serious problem if citizens expected the government alone to meet every need.

4. Some states (are trying/trying) to eliminate bilingual education classes in their schools.

5. Administrators of bilingual programs have not usually (ask/asked) parents and community groups for input.

6. Parents must (involve/to involve) themselves in bilingual programs.

7. Parents who have time should (volunteer/volunteering) with community organizations to propel bilingual education forward.

8. Many people (believe/are believing) that this kind of activism would enable bilingual education to reach its goal.

9. A student could (achieve/achieves) fluency in English with the help of his or her parents.

10. In order to overcome discrimination, citizens must be (unite/united) to solve the language problem.

Exercise 6.13 Verb Phrases

Each of the following sentences contains a verb phrase error. Revise each sentence.

> **Example:** Many people who ~~are~~ study English as a foreign language focus on learning the grammar of written English.

1. Students of English are often surprise by the differences between written and conversational English.

2. Those students who have study formal written English may find conversational English difficult to understand.

3. Students who have recently came to an English-speaking country may have particular trouble with slang vocabulary and expressions.

4. Conversation classes in English supposed to help students become familiar with spoken English by simulating real-life situational dialogues.

5. Students who have not exposed to spoken English can listen to English radio or TV broadcasts to help them learn English.

6. Just listening to spoken English can useful in learning oral speech patterns and intonation.

7. Many students find that listening to songs with English lyrics can helps them learn new vocabulary and expressions.

8. Some students who do not feeling a need to learn spoken English might prefer to listen to radio broadcasts in their native language rather than broadcasts in English.

9. If such students do not make a great effort to learn conversational English, they may never can understand the spoken language well.

10. Students in English classes who may not have working hard on learning spoken English need to understand that an inability to speak and understand English can limit their opportunities.

Exercise 6.14 Simple, Perfect, and Progressive Verb Phrases

For each sentence in the following paragraphs, underline the appropriate verb phrase from the pair in parentheses.

> **Example:** In the past ten years, bottled water (became/<u>has become</u>) increasingly popular in America.

While I (shopped/was shopping) at a grocery store last week, I (counted/was counting) five different brands of bottled water on the shelves. These days, bottled water (costs/is costing) more than carbonated beverages, but many consumers now (feel/are feeling) that good health is worth the greater price.

Nutrition experts (have observed/have been observing) that Americans (consume/have consumed) too much soda and junk food. Prior to these findings, some parents (noticed/have noticed) that their children were more sluggish and inattentive after they (had eaten/were eating) junk food. In many cases, they (had been snacking/have been snacking) at school.

Now nutrition experts insist that children (need/are needing) breakfast before school so that they (do not stop/have not been stopping) at vending machines for sodas or greasy snacks. Because studies (showed/have shown) that students perform better when they eat nutritious foods, some schools (consider/are considering) a ban on certain junk foods and soda machines.

However, many parents (believe/are believing) that good nutrition should be enforced by parents, not schools. They (resent/are resenting) being told by the school administration what not to put in their children's lunch. Based on recent sales of bottled water, it (appears/is appearing) that consumers (make/are making) better nutritional choices.

Exercise 6.15 Simple, Perfect, and Progressive Verb Phrases

Revise each of the following sentences by correcting errors in verb phrases, using simple, perfect, and progressive verb forms where appropriate.

> **Example:** In 1954, the U.S. Supreme Court ~~has~~ desegregated education, declaring that "separate educational facilities are inherently unequal."

1. Since then, the states often challenged the federal government either by ignoring or refusing to implement the decision or by filing court cases.

2. The case of Central High School in Little Rock, Arkansas, has been one of the most famous examples of a state fighting this federal mandate.

3. When the school has opened in September 1957, the Arkansas National Guard was called out to prevent African Americans from entering the school.

4. President Dwight D. Eisenhower ordered the army into Little Rock to enforce the court order, and African American children finally were entering the school with the protection of federal troops.

5. State-supported resistance to desegregation was not ending with the Little Rock case.

6. However, over the years the courts consistently ruled in favor of desegregation.

7. Racial integration of schools is remaining a concern for the current generation as well.

8. Recent statistics are showing that about 35 percent of African American students go to schools in which 90 percent of the student body is nonwhite.

9. In addition, support for integration declines in the current political climate.

10. Today, the fight for desegregation was largely replaced by the fight for quality education for all students.

Participles

Participles are adjectives that have been created from verbs by adding suffixes (for regular verbs, usually *-ed* and *-ing*).

A **participial adjective** is a participle that describes a noun. You can often use the present active and past active participles as adjectives, particularly to describe feelings or actions. The **present participle** describes the thing or person causing the feeling or action. The **past participle** describes the person having the feeling or experiencing the action.

An **interesting** article was in the newspaper today. (present participle: *interesting*)

All **interested** parties were encouraged to apply for the position. (past participle: *interested*)

The **boring** lecture finally came to an end. (present participle: *boring*)

The **bored** student had fallen asleep in his chair by the time class was dismissed. (past participle: *bored*)

The **cutting** remark brought tears to Kate's eyes. (present participle: *cutting*)

The **cut** padlock proved that someone had accessed the storage unit without permission. (past participle: *cut*)

A **frightening** shadow appeared in the doorway. (present participle: *frightening*)

Hearing a loud peal of thunder, the **frightened** girl ran to her mother. (past participle: *frightened*)

Infinitives and Gerunds

While an infinitive is a verb form and functions as a verb, a gerund only *appears* to be a verb (it looks like a progressive form), when in fact it is actually a noun derived from a verb. Choosing between infinitives and gerunds can present difficulties for non-native speakers. Generally, you should use infinitives when stating intentions, desires, or expectations; you should use gerunds to state facts or events.

Sergey **wants to work** at the local coffee shop. (infinitive: *to work*)

Dr. Brenes **started working** on her new book this summer. (gerund: *working*)

However, you should use a gerund, not an infinitive, following a preposition.

A stethoscope is used **for listening** to heartbeats. (gerund: *listening*)

A stethoscope is used **to listen** to heartbeats. (infinitive: *to listen*)

These cookies were made **for eating**. (gerund: *eating*)

These cookies were made **to eat**. (infinitive: to *eat*)

Exercise 6.16 Participles

In each of the following sentences, underline the participles.

   Example: The <u>howling</u> dog awakened everyone at midnight.

1. The flags of the color guard appeared around the corner, signaling the beginning of the parade.

2. The cheering crowd welcomed the first procession of the Mardi Gras season.

3. Thousands of onlookers packed the sides of the downtown streets in anticipation of catching beads and trinkets.

4. Each parading Mardi Gras organization has a different theme each year for its procession.

5. The theme of this particular parade is "Smiling Faces," and each float features a famous comedian.

6. Carrying torch-lit signs, men dressed as court jesters announce the name of each float.

7. Enormous floats slowly pass by as their riders throw beads and plastic cups to the waving crowd.

8. My favorite float was the Charlie Chaplin float, featuring a gigantic rendition of his famous character, the tramp.

9. Ten marching bands, twelve floats crowded with masked revelers, and an entire cast of horses, clowns, and silly characters combine to form the parade.

10. A parade of a different type immediately follows each Mardi Gras parade; rumbling in unison, the street sweeper trucks prepare for their big moment as the last float passes.

Exercise 6.17 Participles

Write the correct participial form of the verb given in parentheses.

Example: The sparrow was _____*singing*_____ (sing) loudly at my window.

1. _____ (Carry) the heavy picnic basket, Joe searched with Nancy for a lovely spot in the park to have lunch.

2. Joe's stomach was _____ (growl) as he reached inside the basket and grabbed a sandwich.

3. He consumed the entire sandwich without Nancy's _____ (notice).

4. "This spot is _____ (overflow) with ants," said Nancy. "Let's try on the other side of the park."

5. _____ (Wander) aimlessly, the couple searched from one end of the park to the other.

6. Joe was _____ (eat) the entire time that it took for them to find the perfect location for their picnic.

7. The _____ (roam) couple at last discovered a shady, dry place with no ants.

8. They both decided that it was the perfect _____ (picnic) spot, and they spread out the blanket.

9. Without _____ (look) into the basket, Nancy reached in to get a sandwich but discovered that the basket was empty.

10. She turned to Joe, who was _____ (finish) the last bit of food that was packed for lunch!

Exercise 6.18 Participial Adjectives

For each of the following sentences, circle the appropriate participial adjective from the pair in parentheses.

> **Example:** One of the most (fascinated/~~fascinating~~) recent developments in medicine is the use of robots in surgery.

1. Many doctors are (excited/exciting) about the advantages robots have over humans in medicine.

2. Of course, a robot will never be able to calm a nervous patient with a (soothed/soothing) explanation of a medical procedure.

3. A (terrified/terrifying) patient about to undergo surgery might prefer a human doctor.

4. However, robot "surgeons" never become (tired/tiring) when standing for hours during an operation.

5. Of course, an (observed/observing) doctor will control the robot's actions.

6. Surgical robots can correct the movements of a doctor's (shaken/shaking) hands.

7. These robots, equipped with cameras, magnifying lenses, and bright lights, allow doctors an (amazed/amazing) view inside the human body without the need for large incisions.

8. Robotic surgical assistance should decrease the number of (horrified/horrifying) problems that can happen during and after surgery because of human errors.

9. Instead, the robots and their human operators can complete surgery with more (satisfied/satisfying) results.

10. Someday, surgical patients may be (surprised/surprising) to learn that their doctor had mechanical assistance during the operation.

Name _____   Section _____ Date _____

Exercise 6.19 Participial Adjectives

Revise any of the following sentences that do not use participial adjectives correctly. If a sentence does not contain an error, write **C** above it.

             astonished

Example: The ~~astonishing~~ medical students could hardly believe the realism of
their new mechanical practice patient.

1. Suffered patients have been used for medical students' practice in teaching hospitals for decades.

2. No matter how interested a student is in medical school lectures, the lectures cannot prepare him or her to perform procedures on patients.

3. Sitting in a packing lecture hall, first- and second-year medical students can only imagine working on a real patient.

4. However, disgusting patients soon tire of having amateurs use them to practice starting IVs, drawing blood, and giving injections.

5. Repeated practice is absolutely necessary for good medical technique, but what patients are willing to let medical students spend hours prodding and poking them?

6. New technologically advanced fiberglass "patients" allow fumbling medical students to practice on them for as long as the students wish.

7. A distressing medical student may choke a mechanical patient repeatedly while trying to put a tube down its throat, and the machine will utter a loud gagging noise.

8. The gagging sound is unnerved, but students' mistakes do not hurt any living human beings.

9. The uncomplained mechanical patients allow students to develop good medical technique before they handle real people.

10. When these teaching techniques become more widespread, hospitalized people all over the United States will be relieving.

Exercise 6.20 Infinitives and Gerunds

For each sentence in the following paragraphs, circle either the infinitive or the gerund given in parentheses.

> **Example:** Anyone who plans (to study/studying) in another country should be aware that university systems differ from place to place.

Since a university education in one country may differ from a university experience in another, students studying outside their native country may struggle (to understand/understanding) educational attitudes within foreign institutions. For example, in some countries students are expected (to avoid/avoiding) (to speak/speaking) in class, but in other countries it is expected, if not required. Moreover, instructors in some countries encourage students (to participate/participating) actively by (to solve/solving) problems in groups, (to make/making) presentations, and (to examine/examining) case studies.

Another aspect of the foreign classroom that is often confusing is the teacher-student relationship. In many countries this relationship is a formal one; in other countries it can appear (to be/being) more relaxed. Regardless of the level of formality between teacher and student, students should remember (to meet/meeting) deadlines for assignments and (to treat/treating) the professor with respect. Even if a professor meets with students outside of class (to have/having) coffee with them, this shouldn't make the professor appear (to be/being) any less of an authority figure.

Exercise 6.21 Infinitives and Gerunds

For each of the following sentences, fill in the blank with the appropriate infinitive or gerund formed from the verb given in parentheses.

> **Example:** It is easy to understand foreign students' _____*being*_____ (be) confused about grades in American university classes.

1. Most U.S. professors prefer their students _____ (work) independently, but professors do offer help to students who need it.

2. University policies forbid students _____ (share) answers on a test.

3. However, instructors often encourage their students _____ (collaborate) in teams on projects other than tests and papers.

4. Universities consider _____ (plagiarize) written work as grounds for expulsion.

5. Dishonest students may jeopardize their relationship with other students who resent their _____ (cheat).

6. Instructors expect students _____ (do) the work for a class even if the work will not be graded.

7. Some teachers believe that not grading an assignment enables students _____ (judge) their own work.

8. If students want to improve their grades, professors often support students' _____ (work) with a tutor.

9. But most professors don't appreciate their students' _____ (ask) about grades on a test or paper in the middle of class.

10. Students who want class time to discuss grades risk _____ (anger) their professors.

Exercise 6.22 Infinitives and Gerunds

Revise each sentence to correct any errors in the use of infinitives and gerunds.

> **Example:** Understanding the nature of competition in an American university is necessary for students ~~succeeding~~ *to* there.

1. International students who are considering to study in the United States should realize that relationships between students here can be either cooperative or competitive, depending on the class.

2. International students who expect cooperating with classmates may initially feel uncomfortable with the competition in American schools.

3. Of course, they should not hesitate asking their classmates for help.

4. In some courses, however, the instructor might decide calculating students' grades in relation to one another.

5. This method of to grade is called a curve.

6. When a curve is used, students may be reluctant sharing their lecture notes with others because they don't want to hurt their own grades.

7. Students without high grade-point averages risk not to get into a top graduate program.

8. Employers trying to fill a job opening may also choose looking at a candidate's grade-point average and faculty recommendations.

9. When students under pressure are asked deciding between helping classmates and decreasing competition for a high grade-point average, they often choose the latter.

10. International students sometimes have to get used to function in this competitive system.

Exercise 6.23 Taking the Next Step with Verbs

Describe a favorite sport or hobby you enjoy. Be sure to use as many of the verb forms and vocabulary you leaned in this chapter as you can. Refer to the relevant sections of this chapter as you work to help you master each concept.

_____

_____

_____

_____

_____

_____

_____

_____

_____

_____

Part 7
Modifiers

Determiners

Determiners are a class of modifiers—words that describe other words. They include the following common words.

The articles **a/an**, **the**

This, these, that, those

My, our, your, his, her, its, their

Whose, which, what

all, both, each, every, some, any, either, no, neither, many, more, most, much, (a) few, (a) little, several, enough

Possessive nouns and noun phrases (**Emily's, her uncle's**)

The numerals **one, two, three**, etc.

Noun phrases containing a singular count noun must begin with a determiner.

the museum

my digital camera

a feather

that brown cow

Noncount and plural count nouns may or may not have determiners, depending on the meaning intended:

Exercise is good for you.	=	Exercise in general is good for you.
This exercise is good for you.	=	This specific exercise is good for you.

When choosing determiners, be sure to remember which determiners go with each type of noun.

this, that   +   **singular count or noncount nouns**

this newspaper, that tea

these, (a) few, many, both, several   +   **plural count nouns**

these eggs, a few students, many examples, both candidates, several packages

(a) little, much   +   **noncount nouns**

a little cream, much trouble

some, enough   +   **noncount or plural count nouns**

some cereal, enough time

a, an, every, each   +   **singular count nouns**

a stereo, an elephant, every person, each day

Exercise 7.1 Determiners

In the following paragraph, underline the determiners. The first sentence has been done for you.

    Historically, Japan has not been <u>a</u> country that encouraged immigration. The current labor shortage, however, may force that country to start allowing immigration. Because of Japan's low birthrate, not enough new workers are entering the workforce. Then, when women do have children, few new mothers stay in the job market. In addition, Japan's population is aging faster than the population of any other developed nation. Soon, four times as many Japanese citizens will be over age sixty-five as will be under that age. For these three reasons, the country will not be able to achieve economic growth or support itself unless it expands its labor pool. What strategy would have a more immediate effect than inviting immigration?

Exercise 7.2 Determiners

For each of the following sentences, underline the appropriate determiner from the pair in parentheses. **X** means "no determiner."

> **Example:** Getting (X/<u>a</u>) good education is the most certain way to get a good job.

1. Many people decide to immigrate to the United States for their (children/children's) education.

2. Immigrant parents must also worry about finding (a/some) job to support their families.

3. There are not (many/much) good opportunities for immigrants who have no education.

4. Often, uneducated immigrants end up getting (X/a) jobs with low pay.

5. They are likely to live in (X/a) poor neighborhood.

6. In the United States, schools get some money for (they/their) budgets from taxes paid in the area.

7. (Many/Much) schools in poor neighborhoods do not have enough money to pay teachers well or to provide good facilities for students.

8. Unfortunately, (X/a) student from a poor neighborhood may have to be exceptionally motivated to get a decent education.

9. (Every/All) children should have an equal opportunity to be educated and find fulfilling work.

10. Perhaps someday (X/this) ideal will become a reality for all of (America/America's) children.

Exercise 7.3 Determiners

Each of the following sentences contains an error in the use of determiners. Revise each sentence by adding, deleting, and changing determiners wherever appropriate.

Example: The average Amcrican is afraid to speak in front of ^*a* group.

1. Much businesses today expect executives to be good public speakers.

2. In fact, person who cannot speak well in public is unlikely to be promoted to an executive position.

3. However, 40 percent of all Americans have terrible fear of public speaking.

4. For these people, giving some speech is usually a miserable experience.

5. Experts suggest a little ways to help conquer a fear of public speaking.

6. Taking few deep breaths before a speech gives the speaker extra oxygen and can calm nerves.

7. Some speakers feel more confident when they imagine the audience in they underwear.

8. When speakers remember something that made them laugh recently, funny memory can help them to relax.

9. People who have an extreme problems with public speaking might need professional help.

10. Many organizations can help to conquer a businessperson fear of giving speeches.

Exercise 7.4 Modifiers

Underline the appropriate modifier from the pair in parentheses.

Example: The teacher awarded prizes to (any, <u>a few</u>) of the students.

Some people believe that having (1.) (any, a few) sweets in your diet will not harm your health. Others say that even (2.) (a little, a few) bit of sugar can be harmful. Most people will admit that not eating (3.) (a little, any) sweets is very hard to do. But there are (4.) (a few, any) things you can do to maintain a healthy body and satisfy a sugar craving. One way is to just eat (5.) (a few, a little) bit of a dessert, and not the entire portion. Another thing you can do is avoid (6.) (any, a little) sweet that is extremely high in sugar and fat, and pick a sweet that has more natural sugars and fewer calories. If you are trying to lose weight, you should avoid eating (7.) (a little, any) sweets for a short period of time so your body becomes used to living without sugar. You might be motivated to stick to your diet if you lose (8.) (a little, a few) pounds. The hardest part about cutting back on your sugar intake is that after a while (9.) (any, a few) dessert will be tempting. Like most things, though, moderation is key: don't torture yourself; have (10.) (a little, a few) bit of dessert.

Exercise 7.5 Modifiers

Fill in each blank with the correct modifier. Use **a few**, **a little**, or **any**.

> **Example:** I didn't read _____**any**_____ books over the summer.

1. The bookstore manager placed an order for _____ books on making stained glass and one special book on antiques from ABC Books.

2. The books were expected to arrive in _____ days.

3. When the books didn't arrive by Saturday, the manager knew the books would be arriving _____ late.

4. The manager called the warehouse, but he didn't get _____ answer about why the books were late.

5. _____ bit later, the warehouse supervisor called back to say that a few other bookstores had also not received their orders.

6. He said he didn't know of _____ reason that the books were not delivered.

7. Finally, on Tuesday _____ delivery trucks arrived to drop off the book shipment.

8. Instead of receiving a few books on stained glass, the bookstore didn't receive _____ books on stained glass.

9. Also, instead of receiving one special book on antiques, the bookstore received quite _____ books on antiques.

10. The bookstore manager decided that the next time he ordered books, he would order from _____ store other than ABC Books.

Exercise 7.6 Modifiers

Underline the appropriate modifier from the pair in parentheses.

    Example: The problem with (much, <u>some</u>) laptop computers is that they are too heavy.

    (1.) (Much, Many) student athletes go on to university if they receive an athletic scholarship. There are (2.) (many, much) universities that recruit the best athletes from high schools around the country. There is (3.) (many, much) controversy surrounding athletes who get preferential treatment in their academic courses if they are not doing well. (4.) (Much, Some) universities, but not all, have a "no pass, no play" policy. This policy means that if a student does not "pass" an academic course, he cannot "play" in the sports program. This policy not only affects the athlete, it also affects (5.) (much, many) professors. (6.) (Much, Some) professors understand the demands of an athlete's life among practice, training, and games. Others believe that athletes receive too (7.) (some, many) privileges and should be treated just like other students. Even other students say that the athletes get too (8.) (many, much) preferential treatment. In addition, corporate sponsors promote (9.) (much, many) sports and athletes because they recognize the potential income an athlete might bring. There is (10.) (some, much) to be said for how a corporate sponsorship can change an athlete's life.

Exercise 7.7 Modifiers

Circle the appropriate modifier from the pair in parentheses.

> **Example:** Carpets and rugs from ((some,) any) parts of the world are woven by hand.

1. Automobile manufacturers in the United States face competition from (some, any) of the other big automobile makers around the world.

2. If you look at (some, any) one manufacturer, you will find a variety of vehicles introduced every year.

3. Manufacturers attempt to reach consumers with flashy advertising; (any, some) consumers are influenced by the advertising, while others are not.

4. The budget-conscious consumer might say that (some, any) car will do.

5. For (any, some) consumers, the reliability of a vehicle is the most important factor.

6. Others might choose a car based on (some, any) outstanding features such as design, leather interiors, or computerized controls.

7. (Any, Some) manufacturers offer customized cars for their more wealthy customers.

8. With so many choices, it is hard to say which, if (some, any), car is the best.

9. One thing is for certain: (some, any) car(s) must meet certain safety regulations.

10. Here is (any, some) advice: test-drive any car before you buy.

Exercise 7.8 Modifiers

Circle the appropriate modifier from the pair in parentheses.

Example: I wanted to buy (that, (those)) shoes, but the other customer picked them up first.

1. The librarian put (these, this) dictionary in the rare books room.

2. The rare books are stored in (that, those) bookcases with glass doors.

3. The dictionary came from an estate sale on (this, these) side of town.

4. Other rare books are stored in (these, this) room.

5. The oldest books are (this, these) books of maps.

6. They were not published in (this, these) century.

7. Another interesting item in the room is (those, that) wooden globe in the corner.

8. The globe is also from (those, that) older century.

9. All of (these, this) books are so rare that they are treated with very special care.

10. When you surround yourself with these books, you might forget that you live in (these, this) century.

Exercise 7.9 Modifiers

Circle the correct modifier from the pair in parentheses.

Example: She painted (these, this) portraits five years ago.

1. Every year, more and more people move to (these, this) part of the city.

2. The reason people like to live here is because of all (this, these) beautiful parks.

3. They also like all (that, those) old oak trees.

4. We didn't know (these, this) neighborhood would become so popular.

5. In fact, (that, those) school was built because so many young parents moved here two years ago.

6. All of (this, these) children walk to their school because it is nearby.

7. The school colors and mascots are on (that, those) flags.

8. We were not surprised when (that, those) big blue house was sold in one day.

9. We have thought about moving to (that, those) side of town where it is more rural.

10. One day, we will sell (this, these) house and move to a smaller one.

Exercise 7.10 Modifiers

Fill in each blank with the correct modifier, using **this** or **these**.

Example: He took care of _____this_____ lawn all summer.

1. _____ store sells fine furniture made from real wood.

2. First, the sales associate showed us _____ dressers and beds, which are made from oak.

3. I am more interested in _____ bed, which is made from cherry.

4. _____ dresser matches the bed and bedside tables.

5. The most beautiful bedroom sets are in _____ rooms in the rear of the building.

6. _____ sets also cost twice as much as the other sets.

7. The other thing that I am looking at is _____ living room set.

8. I like _____ sofa because it is made out of leather.

9. I also like it because I found _____ pillows to coordinate with it.

10. _____ might be the last furniture store I will have to look in.

Adjectives

Adjectives are a type of modifier that modify nouns—they number, limit, describe, or otherwise specify what kind of noun you are referring to. They answer the questions *Which?* and *What kind of?*

> The **red** balloon
>
> An **overstuffed** armchair
>
> The **large** pizza
>
> This **difficult algebra** problem

In English, adjectives usually precede the noun they describe. Adjectives that are separated from the noun they describe by a linking verb or another verb that functions similarly are **predicate adjectives**.

> That dress is **lovely**.
>
> Those eggs smell **rotten**.
>
> Those decorations seem **ostentatious**.
>
> The fox was **quick**.

Many adjectives have comparative and superlative forms as well.

Adjective	Comparative	Superlative
bad	worse	worst
big	bigger	biggest
far	farther	farthest
good	better	best
happy	happier	happiest
sad	sadder	saddest
smart	smarter	smartest

Correct modifier placement can present a challenge for non-native speakers of English. Consider the sequence of modifiers in the sentence below.

> That tired, hungry, sad-looking big old brown English hunting dog with the spot on his back looks like he could use a good home.

Here are some general guidelines to keep in mind when using more than one modifier for a noun. You might think it would be impossible to figure out how to choose the correct word order in the sentence above, but a few basic guidelines can help.

1. Determiners go at the very beginning of the phrase.

   > **That** dog

   All or *both* precedes any other determiners (<u>*both*</u> those dogs); numbers follow any other determiners (those <u>*two*</u> dogs).

2. Phrases or clauses follow the noun.

   > That dog **with the spot on his back**.

3. Noun modifiers go right before the noun they modify.

   > That **hunting** dog with the spot on his back

4. Any other adjectives go between determiners and noun modifiers.

   That **old** hunting dog with the spot on his back

In cases of two or more adjectives (not including the determiners and noun modifiers), the order is variable, but the following guidelines may be helpful.

1. Subjective adjectives (those that express the speaker's opinions and attitudes) come earlier than objective adjectives (those that express facts or descriptions).

   That **sad-looking** old hunting dog with the spot on his back

2. Adjectives denoting size generally come earlier in the phrase.

   That sad-looking **big** old hunting dog with the spot on his back

3. Adjectives denoting color usually come later.

   That sad-looking big old **brown** hunting dog with the spot on his back

4. Adjectives derived from proper nouns usually come in the middle.

   That sad-looking big old brown **English** hunting dog with the spot on his back

5. Other objective adjectives come in the middle. If the phrase includes more than one adjective for which no particular order exists, you should separate the adjectives with commas.

   That **tired, hungry, sad-looking** big old brown English hunting dog with the spot on his back

While the cumbersome phrase above helps to demonstrate the preferred order for modifiers, it is rare in English. These kinds of wordy constructions are difficult to understand; you should avoid them in your own writing.

Adverbs

Adverbs are a type of modifier that modify verbs, adjectives, other adverbs, or entire clauses. They answer the question *How? Why? When? Where?* or *To what degree?* You can form many adverbs from adjectives by adding *-ly* to the end of the adjective.

Adjective	Adverb
quick	quickly
thoughtless	thoughtlessly
great	greatly
fashionable	fashionably
reasonable	reasonably
strident	stridently
bright	brightly
poor	poorly

However, not all adverbs end in *-ly*, and some adjectives end in *-ly* (*friendly, lovely*). Some common adverbs not ending in *-ly* include *more, most, always, never, not, very, too,* and *much.* Also note that the adverb form of the adjective *good* is *well,* not *goodly.*

A few adverbs, such as *fast* and *far*, have forms identical to the adjective.

That car is going **much too fast** in this neighborhood.

The adverb *fast* modifies *is going*, *too* modifies *fast*, and *much* modifies *too*.

Far too many people were crammed into the elevator.

The determiner *many* modifies the noun *people*, the adverb *too* modifies *many*, and the adverb *far* modifies *too*.

Many adverbs can also be used to make comparisons.

apprehensively   **more** apprehensively   **most** apprehensively

Some adverbs modify entire clauses and help to connect the meaning between that clause and the preceding one. Examples include *also, consequently, furthermore, however, likewise, therefore,* and *thus*.

It rained all day yesterday; **consequently**, the picnic was cancelled.

Name _____ Section _____ Date _____

Exercise 7.11 Adjectives

Underline the adjective, and draw an arrow from the adjective to the word that it modifies.

Example: Murky water bubbled into the boat through the hole in its hull.

1. The tattered jersey hangs from the rafters of the gymnasium.

2. A faded number eight and the name "McCormick" are on the back of it.

3. On the front of the jersey is our school mascot, a dragon.

4. The legend of the jersey is told to all students at the beginning of the year

5. Years ago, the Dragons were losing a basketball game.

6. It was the final game of the season, and Rod McCormick had never played.

7. Rod was the shortest member of the team.

8. When a star player was injured, the coach put Rod in the game.

9. Rod managed to land an unbelievable shot at the buzzer, winning the game.

10. The next day, the coach hung the jersey from the rafters to remind everyone of the terrific game.

130 • *Part 7 / Modifiers*

Exercise 7.12 Adjectives

Underline each adjective, and draw an arrow to the word that it modifies. There may be more than one adjective in each sentence.

Example: The car sped down the gravel road.

1. The overstuffed backpack dangled from a hook by the door of the library.

2. Ellen glanced guiltily at the backpack over the top of a fashion magazine.

3. "Ellen, you'd better get started," said Amy. "The research paper is due on Friday."

4. Shooting Amy a dirty look, Ellen retrieved the backpack.

5. She unzipped the flap so that she could search for her rough draft.

6. The backpack was an unruly mess, filled with books, paper, pens, and an old sandwich.

7. Finally, Ellen found the crumpled draft at the bottom of the backpack.

8. Smoothing the paper out on the table, Ellen realized that Friday was only two days away.

9. Working diligently, she was able to finish the paper, but it was not her best work.

10. When Friday arrived, Ellen turned in the paper knowing that next time, she would not procrastinate.

Name _____ Section _____ Date _____

Exercise 7.13 Adjectives

Revise each of the following sentences to correct any errors in the arrangement of adjectives.

        Example: Attention deficit disorder, or A.D.D., results from a ~~problem chemical~~ *chemical problem* in the brain.

1. Most people with attention deficit disorder display behavioral obvious symptoms such as hyperactivity, disorganization, impulsiveness, and an inability to manage time effectively.

2. These all symptoms affect performance in certain jobs.

3. A.D.D. was once thought to exist only in troublesome a few children, but now experts believe that adults can also suffer from it.

4. Nowadays, new research and openness about the condition help prevent job potential discrimination.

5. Most adults would have trouble remaining completely focused on a thirty-minute boring slide presentation.

6. For an adult with A.D.D., such a task is a cognitive huge burden.

7. Modifications simple in the work routine can help A.D.D. sufferers to be more effective in their job.

8. Organizing paperwork by color and size clears up kinds of some confusion for A.D.D. sufferers.

9. For example, a green large folder might contain invoices, and a small blue folder could hold receipts.

10. If it is not possible for them to change office daily confusing routines, A.D.D. sufferers should consider changing careers.

Exercise 7.14 Adjectives

Read the passage below, and use adjectives from the word list to complete the sentences. The first blank has been filled in for you.

Word List
black   vegetable   faded   neglected   young   delicious   neat   early   beautiful

The _____black_____ crow called loudly from the shoulder of the _____

scarecrow. The _____ garden had not been tended in years. Vegetables no

longer grew in _____ rows, because weeds and briars had taken their places.

In _____ autumn, the house was put up for sale. One day, a car pulled into the

driveway, and a _____ couple got out. They immediately loved the house and

its garden. "This is perfect!" said the man to his _____ wife, and she agreed.

They bought the house and began to tend the _____ garden at once. By sum-

mertime, the house was once again lovely, and vegetables were again growing in the

_____ garden.

Exercise 7.15 Adjectives

Read the passage below, and use adjectives from the word list to complete the sentences. The first blank has been filled in for you.

Word List

thrilling   interesting   several   frightening   hard
layered   next   brave   early   additional

The origin of the roller coaster is an ___interesting___ one. _____ roller

coasters, in fact, did not roll at all. They were slides made from _____ wood

and then covered with _____ sheets of ice. _____ riders would

climb stairs leading up to the back of the slides. Once at the top, the passengers would

rocket down the _____ 50 degree drop and then climb an _____

set of stairs leading to the _____ slide. These _____ slides were a

favorite of Catherine the Great, and legend has it that she had _____ slides

constructed on her estate to entertain guests.

Exercise 7.16 Adverbs

Underline the adverb, and draw an arrow to the word that it modifies.

> **Example:** The students listened <u>carefully</u> to the directions before starting the exam.

1. Robert slowly turned the doorknob.

2. The door creaked eerily as Robert peered into the parlor.

3. "Grandma," called Robert loudly, "it's Tuesday—are you ready to go?"

4. Mrs. Stadler finally answered, "Yes, Bobby, I'm packing my shoes now."

5. By 1 P.M., Robert and his grandma were walking briskly to the studio.

6. They regularly spent Tuesday afternoons together.

7. Tuesdays were affectionately known as "dancing days."

8. Grandma thoroughly enjoyed dancing with Robert because it reminded her of dancing with his grandfather.

9. Grandpa Ken had died suddenly last year.

10. Robert especially enjoyed spending time with his grandma and filling in for Grandpa Ken.

Exercise 7.17 Adverbs

Fill in the blanks with an appropriate adverb from the word list. The first blank has been filled in for you.

Word List

fortunately   graciously   extremely   calmly   today
especially   nervously   fast   supposedly   recently

Gus University is ____extremely____ proud of its men's track team, _____

the star of the team, Andre. Andre runs very _____ . In fact, he

_____ set a new record at Gus U for the 50 yard dash. _____ he is

competing in the state meet. _____ , Olympic scouts are coming to watch him

run. Coach Vasquez will be looking around _____ , trying to detect the scouts.

_____ , Andre is more focused than his coach. _____ , he will

stretch his legs, arms, and body in preparation for his main event, the 50 yard dash. If

Andre wins, he will _____ accept the handshakes of Coach Vasquez and me,

the incognito Olympic scout.

Exercise 7.18 Adverbs

Underline the adverb in each sentence, and draw an arrow to the word that it modifies.

Example: The audience could not hear the <u>softly</u> spoken words.

1. Leigh quickly put on her hiking boots and grabbed her duffle bag.

2. Her mom had been waiting patiently for her in the van.

3. "Here's my archeologist," Mrs. White said proudly as Leigh climbed into the passenger seat.

4. The van made its way speedily across town to the Museum of Natural Science.

5. When Leigh and her mom arrived at the museum, the curator promptly met them at the back door.

6. "Do you have it with you?" the curator asked excitedly.

7. Leigh knowingly patted the duffle bag and nodded yes.

8. The curator led them to a brightly lit room filled with spectators, and he introduced Leigh to the crowd.

9. He said, "My fellow archeologists, you have all heard of the rare specimen of prehistoric bone discovered recently by Leigh White. She has come to show us her find."

10. The crowd applauded wildly as Leigh lifted the bone for all to see.

Exercise 7.19 Adverbs

Read the passage below. Use adverbs from the word list to complete the sentences. The first blank has been filled in for you.

Word List

actively   anxiously   eagerly   traditionally   quickly   consistently   recently   fiercely

___Traditionally___ , in this school district, Field Day is a competition among local high

schools. Every year, students _____ await it. Our coaches talked about team

spirit and sportsmanship, but even so the events are _____ competitive. They

include track and field events as well as a tug of war. The events move _____ .

Competitors _____ wait for their scores. Murray High School has

_____ won Field Day, so of course everyone wants to beat them. But this year

might be their year to lose. A new event has _____ been added: a poster con-

test. It means that even nonathletic students can _____ participate in Field

Day. The winning poster is will be awarded 100 points. Who knows, maybe this year

Murray High School can be stopped.

Exercise 7.20 Taking the Next Step with Modifiers

Describe the most beautiful, scary, interesting, or unusual place you've ever been. What does it look like? Where is it? What can you do there? Be sure to use modifiers, adjectives, adverbs, and the vocabulary you learned in this chapter. Refer to the relevant sections of this chapter as you work to help you master each concept.

_____

_____

_____

_____

_____

_____

_____

_____

_____

_____

Part 8
Prepositions

Prepositions are words that show the relationship between other words. Notice how the meaning of the first sentence below changes when the prepositions are rearranged.

Dave went **from** the university **to** work **with** them.

Dave went **to** the university **with** work **from** them.

Prepositions are followed by a noun or pronoun to form a **prepositional phrase**.

to the university

between them

with my friend

from a big city

for me

When the preposition *to* is followed by a verb in its base form, the two words form the infinitive verb form (*to work*).

Using English prepositions correctly can be especially difficult for ESL writers, because there is no one-to-one correspondence in prepositional usage between languages and usage is sometimes idiomatic. Generally, the use of different prepositions will change the meaning. But in a few cases, you can use different prepositions to express the same thought.

The discussion was **about** the use of the Internet.

The discussion was **on** the use of the Internet.

The discussion was **over** the use of the Internet.

Using *At, In, On*

Using the prepositions *at*, *in*, and *on* correctly can be particularly challenging. Here are some guidelines and examples to help you in using these three prepositions.

Expressions of Time

Preposition	Used to express	Examples
At	specific times	*at midnight,* *at 5:26 P.M.* *at eleven o'clock* *at six*
In	general times or periods of time	*in February* *in 1972* *in the afternoon* *in the meantime* *in these years*

On	specific days and dates	*on Saturday* *on June 23* *on Valentine's Day* *on my birthday*

Expressions of Place

Preposition	Used to express	Examples
At	presence at a specific place or event, or participation in some event	*at the local library* *at a movie theater* *at the tennis match* *at the doctor's office*
In	location inside an enclosed area or an area with specific boundaries	*in the yard* *in my car* *in a bookstore* *in the pool* *in a box* *in an envelope* *in a tree*
On	one object supported by another object with some surface of both objects touching each other	*on that table* *on the road* *on her finger* *on your face* *on the roof* *on a branch*

Below are more examples to help you compare the different uses of *at, in*, and *on*.

At	In	On
at work	in the office	on the job
at the stadium	in the bleachers	on the football field
at the game	in the crowd	on the court
at the zoo	in the aquarium	on the iceberg
at two P.M.	in April	on Tuesday
at nine o'clock	in October	on July 19th
at midnight	in 1968	on September 13, 2003
at night	in the bed	on a mattress

Abstract Usage

It is usually harder to know which prepositions to use in an abstract sense than which ones to use to express physical location. In some contexts, you can derive abstract usage from the literal "physical" meaning, but often this may seem arbitrary.

Manuel is **in** agreement **with** Yalila about this.

Imagine that Manuel is standing next to (*with*) Yalila on this issue; they are in the same place in terms of their opinions.

Here are other examples of *at*, *in*, and *on* used in an abstract sense.

At   *at a loss, at sixes and sevens, at odds*
In   *in love, in a fix, in pain, in a state of confusion, in agreement*
On   *on edge, on guard, on target, on task, on time*

It is best to learn prepositions as you encounter them in different contexts, and little by little you will begin to understand the scope of their use.

Exercise 8.1 Prepositions

For each of the following sentences, underline the appropriate preposition from the pair in parentheses. **X** means "no preposition."

> **Example:** Most (<u>X</u>/of) teenagers in the United States work part-time jobs during the school year.

1. Teenagers want to show (X/to) people that they can stand on their own two feet.

2. Because they crave independence, teenagers don't want their families taking care (to/of) them financially.

3. Many adults don't agree (to/with) this idea; they believe that working diminishes precious study time.

4. Not only can working interfere (in/with) schoolwork, but it can also negatively affect teenagers' health.

5. When I was (in/at) high school, my best friend, an excellent student, took a part-time job.

6. She thought she could handle both work and school, but (in/on) fact, she did not have enough time to do her homework.

7. Her grade-point average fell (on/from) 3.95 (to/on) 2.40.

8. Her parents finally objected (to/on) the amount of time she spent at work.

9. The choices teenagers make (in/at) these years will affect the rest of their lives.

10. Teenagers are sometimes confused (on/about) their priorities: are they first and foremost students or workers?

Exercise 8.2 Prepositions

Revise each of the following sentences so that prepositions are used correctly.

      Example: Some people argue that work has a positive influence ~~in~~ ᵒⁿ teenagers.

1. Some parents don't make any effort to understand to teenagers.

2. At such situations, the workplace can provide a place for teens to interact with adult role models.

3. At work, teenagers can learn to form relationships between other people.

4. While they are in high school, students spend a lot of time to their friends or in class.

5. Work, in the other hand, often requires teenagers to cooperate with people they may not know or like very well.

6. Working also gives students something to do at the hours after school.

7. Teenagers with nothing to do after school are more likely to get at trouble.

8. A part-time job can allow teens to pay leisure activities that they would otherwise be unable to afford.

9. Having a little money to spend in things they want or need makes teenagers feel more independent.

10. A teenager's ability to succeed both as a student and as a worker depends largely in his or her sense of responsibility.

Exercise 8.3 Prepositions

Underline the correct preposition to complete each sentence in the paragraph.

Example: Vince hit the baseball (down, <u>through</u>) the windowpane.

Frank Stoeber is responsible (for, by) one of the greatest roadside attractions (below, in) the state of Kansas. A farmer (except, by) trade, Frank would save pieces of string by rolling them (into, past) a ball. The more string that Frank would add, the larger the ball would grow. Instead of using the ball of string (for, over) other projects, Frank continued to add (with, to) it. When Frank donated the ball of string to the town (of, through) Cawker City, it was enormous. (Over, Across) one and one half million feet of string was rolled (toward, within) an 11-foot-wide ball. It was the largest ball of string in Kansas. To ward (upon, off) any potential record breakers, Cawker City holds an annual Twine-A-Thon so that the famous ball of string started by Frank Stoeber can continue to grow.

Exercise 8.4 Prepositions

Fill in each blank with the correct preposition.

> **Example:** The gymnast clutched the medal _____*near*_____ her heart as she waved to the crowd.

1. There are many proverbial sayings _____ American culture.

2. One of them is "There is more than one way _____ skin a cat."

3. This phrase means that there are multiple ways _____ completing a task.

4. Another saying is, "Let's run it _____ the flagpole, and see who salutes."

5. This phrase means to tell your idea to a group of people and listen to feedback _____ the group.

6. The saying "It's easier to go _____ instead of up" relates to motivation.

7. It means that the simple way is to give up and not work _____ a goal.

8. "Keep your eye _____ the ball" is regularly used in the workplace.

9. It refers to the ability to stay focused _____ pressure.

10. Every culture has proverbial sayings _____ its particular language, and they reflect wisdom in words.

Idiomatic Verbs

Some verbs require a specific preposition or prepositions and are idiomatic; these verbs are also called **two-word** or **phrasal verbs**. Examine the following sentences.

> The customer forgot to pay and **walked <u>out the door</u>**.
>
> As soon as the sun was up, the cowboy **set <u>out</u>**.

The first sentence is what you would expect from an intransitive verb followed by a prepositional phrase. Given the definition and general usage of the words *walk* and *out*, their use here and the meaning that they convey aren't surprising. But notice that in the second sentence the preposition does not introduce a prepositional phrase, nor can it be separated from the verb and retain its meaning in this context: as soon as the sun was up, the cowboy left for some unspecified destination. Here the preposition functions as an **adverbial particle**.

While you generally cannot separate intransitive phrasal verbs from their adverbial particles, some transitive phrasal verbs with direct objects can be separated from their particles by the object. The following examples show two ways to express the same idea using a transitive phrasal verb with a direct object.

> Would you **take down** her phone number?
>
> Would you **take** her phone number **down**?

When a pronoun is the direct object of a transitive phrasal verb that can be separated from its particle, it must separate the verb from its particle.

> I'll get a pencil and **take** it **down**.

Not all idiomatic verbs are phrasal verbs, however. **Prepositional verbs** also consist of a verb and a preposition that cannot be separated, but (unlike the adverbial particle in a phrasal verb) the preposition appears to introduce a prepositional phrase. See the sentence below.

> My son **takes after** his father.

Here the words *takes after* cannot be separated from each other and still retain their contextual meaning, but *after* seems to introduce a prepositional phrase (*after his father*). Yet the phrase *after his father* means something different in this context than you might expect: the writer is saying that the son resembles his father in some way, either in physical appearance or in behavior. This class of idiomatic verbs also includes those verbs whose meaning is predictable but whose accompanying preposition is less predictable (*approve of*, *listen to*).

Some idiomatic verbs consist of three words. These **phrasal-prepositional verbs** combine **verb + adverbial particle + prepositional sequence** to create sentences such as the ones below.

> I won't **put up <u>with</u>** his tardiness any longer.
>
> He won't **get away <u>with</u>** that.
>
> We **look forward <u>to</u>** seeing you at the family reunion.

Because of the unpredictability of these verbs (in terms of both the preposition the verb requires and the altered meaning that results from their combination), you must learn them on a case-by-case basis. It is best to memorize and practice them as you encounter them in context.

Use the list of commonly used idiomatic verbs in Appendix C, p. 162, to help you complete the following exercises.

Exercise 8.5 Idiomatic Verbs

For each of the following sentences, underline the appropriate word from the pair in parentheses.

> **Example:** When I think (<u>back to</u>/with) my first day of college, I remember that it did not go very well.

1. It started when I woke (up/on) much later than I should have.

2. I took (up/off) for my first class quickly, without even combing my hair.

3. The class was in a building far from my apartment so I wanted to figure (up/out) a shortcut across the campus.

4. I was about (with/to) cross a lawn on the east side of the campus when I saw the sign that said, "Do not walk on the grass."

5. I didn't want to make anyone angry, but I also wanted to save time, so I ended (by/up) walking across the lawn in spite of the sign's warning.

6. I was nervous about trespassing but I also hoped that I would get away (with/by) it.

7. When I reached the other side of the lawn, I ran (to/into) a security guard coming down the footpath.

8. I started to sweat but decided that I had to put (up with/down with) whatever reprimand he gave me—just hoped that he would not make me later for class.

9. It turned (out/on) that he had not seen me at all.

10. I arrived at class 15 minutes late and immediately began to take (down/up) everything the instructor said.

Exercise 8.6 Idiomatic Verbs

Underline the appropriate word to complete the two-word verb from the pair in parentheses.

> **Example:** During the past ten years, casual dress has caught (<u>on</u>/up) in corporate America.

1. At first, many companies laid (in/out) guidelines for casual dress on Fridays only.

2. Most companies said that employees only had to dress (up/out) on Fridays if they were meeting clients.

3. There were a few problems, though; for example, what if you ran (into/on) a client on casual Friday unexpectedly?

4. Also, for men, the guidelines often meant simply putting (on/off) khakis and a shirt without a tie.

5. However, for women, it was more difficult to figure (on/out) what was casual but not too casual.

6. Nevertheless, companies tried (on/out) casual Fridays first, and now they are making the whole week casual.

7. Employees will soon wake (up/out) to find that they have a whole closet of useless formal clothes.

8. Will Brooks Brothers close (up/down)?

9. Then employees who are building a new wardrobe will have to start (on/over).

10. So, who gets something (out/off) of the change to casual dress? Casual clothing companies, of course.

Exercise 8.7 Idiomatic Verbs

Each of the following sentences contains an error in the use of idiomatic verbs. Rewrite each sentence.

> **Example:** I used get ~~across~~ *along* with the smoking crowd.

1. My idea was that kids who smoked cigarettes turned on to be the coolest kids in school.

2. They came off with unusual things to say and they wore cool clothes.

3. I admired them so much that I would go up with whatever they said we should think or do.

4. One day I put up my coolest clothes and decided to try a cigarette, too.

5. I looked down to being more like them.

6. But when I tried it, the cigarette tasted so disgusting that I wanted to throw on.

7. I started to look at those kids in a new way, and I no longer wanted to take up them.

8. They did not seem to notice that I did not want to hang up with them anymore.

9. I realized that I had put off with their silly ideas for a long time.

10. From that day on, I decided to stick on friends who did not try so hard to be cool.

Exercise 8.8 Taking the Next Step with Prepositions

Write about a recent excursion you took and the sightseeing you did. OR Plan and write about a trip you'd like to take in the future. Where would you like to visit? What would you like to see? When would you like to go? How will you get there? Be sure to use prepositions carefully. Refer to the relevant sections of this chapter as you work to help you master each concept.

_____

_____

_____

_____

_____

_____

_____

_____

_____

Appendix A
Glossary

abstract usage Abstract usage refers to the use of prepositions in a nonconcrete, nonphysical sense. In the sentence *The book is on the table*, the preposition *on* is used to show the physical location of the book. Now consider the sentence *The book is on Dostoevsky*. We know that the book is not literally sitting on the author Dostoevsky, but rather that the book discusses Dostoevsky. In this sentence, the preposition *on* is used in an abstract (nonphysical) sense to indicate the subject of the book.

adjective An adjective is a word that modifies a noun or a noun phrase. Adjectives number, limit, describe, or otherwise specify the kind of noun. *I found five small stainless steel flathead screws lying in the bottom of my desk drawer.*

adjective clause An adjective clause modifies a noun, but unlike other modifiers, an adjective clause comes after the noun it modifies. It may or may not use a relative pronoun such as *that*, *which*, or *who*. *The person who stood behind me at the drugstore had a cold.*

adverb An adverb is a word that modifies a verb, an adjective, another adverb, or a clause. Many adverbs are formed by adding *-ly* to the end of an adjective. *He quickly ran out the door to catch the bus.*

adverbial particle An adverbial particle is a word that looks like a preposition but functions as an adverb when used in conjunction with the appropriate verb. Together the verb and its accompanying adverbial particle become a type of idiomatic verb called a phrasal verb. *She got over her illness quickly.* See Part 8, Prepositions, on p. 141, for more examples of phrasal verbs and their particles.

article The articles *a/an* and *the* (also called article adjectives) belong to a class of modifiers called determiners. You should use the indefinite article *a/an* when you do not expect the reader to know the identity of the noun being modified. (*An* is a variant of *a*. It is used directly before a word beginning with a vowel sound.) You should use the definite article *the* when you do expect the reader to know the noun's identity, or when you are about to reveal it. *A bird flew across the sky.* The identity of the bird is unknown—it has just been introduced to the reader—so the indefinite article is used. There is only one sky, so the definite article is used.

auxiliary verb Also called helping verbs, auxiliary verbs combine with other verbs (usually *be*, *do*, and *have*) to indicate tense, voice, mood, and type of action. *He will have been waiting at the airport for three hours by the time her plane finally arrives.*

base form The base form is the simplest form of verb, with no grammatical endings. *Go.*

clause A clause is a group of words containing a subject and a verb. Some clauses are dependent clauses, meaning that they cannot stand alone as a sentence; other clauses are independent clauses, because they can function independently as a sentence.

comparative form The comparative form is an adjective or adverb used in making comparisons between two things. Comparative adjectives usually end in *-er*. Comparative adverbs are often formed from adjectives by adding the modifier *more* before the adjective. *She is taller than her husband. You should dress more appropriately the next time you go out in the rain.*

complex-compound sentence A sentence that is both complex and compound is a complex-comppound sentence. *Since my father was tired of driving, he stopped at a motel and we spent the night there in Tucumcari.*

complex sentence In a complex sentence, a dependent clause is joined to an independent clause. *Since my father was tired of driving, he stopped at a motel.*

compound sentence In a compound sentence, two independent clauses are joined by a coordinating conjunction. You can create a compound sentence from two separate sentences. *My father stopped at a motel, and we spent the night there in Tucumcari.*

conjunction A conjunction is a word that joins other words, phrases, clauses, or sentences. Types of conjunctions include coordinating conjunctions, correlative conjunctions, and subordinating conjunctions. *She bought a gallon of milk and two dozen jelly doughnuts.*

context Literally meaning "with text," context refers to the situation in which something occurs, is spoken, or is written—in other words, the text that surrounds the text. The context of any given expression is vital for interpreting it.

contextual The adjective form of the noun *context* (see definition above).

contraction A contraction is a word with a letter or letters omitted, usually indicated by an apostrophe. *It's = It is.*

coordinating conjunction A coordinating conjunction joins two or more nouns, pronouns, verbs, adjectives, adverbs, prepositions, conjunctions, phrases, or clauses. Coordinating conjunctions include the words *and, but, or, nor, yet, for, so. He wanted to go bowling, but he preferred to see a movie.*

correlative conjunction A correlative conjunction is a paired conjunction that joins equal elements of a sentence: *both/and, not only/but also, just as/so, either/or, neither/nor, whether/or. Either he's telling the truth or he isn't.*

count noun Count nouns are used where it is reasonably possible to individually count the items that the noun names. *Who ate all the cookies?*

definite article The definite article *the* goes before a noun whose identity is expected to be known to the reader or is about to be revealed. In some cases, the noun is named earlier in the sentence. In other cases, the knowledge is inferred. You can also use *the* with superlative forms and with ordinal numerals (*the first, the sixth*, etc.). *The student looking at the map appears to be lost.* The phrase *looking at the map* tells which student the speaker is referring to, so *the* is used.

dependent clause A dependent clause cannot stand alone as a sentence. Often dependent clauses are independent clauses preceded by a subordinating conjunction. *After the ball game was over, we all went out to eat pizza.*

determiner Determiners are a class of modifiers and include the following common words: *a/an, the; this, these, that, those; my, our, your, his, her, its, their;* possessive nouns and noun phrases *(Emily's, her uncle's); whose, which, what; all, both, each, every, some, any, either, no, neither, many, more, most, much, (a) few, (a) little, several, enough;* the numerals *one, two, three,* etc.

direct object A direct object is the noun, noun phrase, or pronoun that follows a transitive verb and receives the action of the verb. *The dog bit the intruder.*

formal speech/writing Formal speech and writing pay strict attention to grammatical standards and correct spelling, avoiding colloquial expressions and slang. Sentences may have a great deal of subordination. Formal writing, which is more likely to use longer words of Latin or Greek derivation than informal writing, appears in places such as academic journals and textbooks. You may hear formal speech in court cases or in speeches by public officials; these kinds of speeches are almost always written before they are delivered. Formal speech and writing require more attentiveness from both the writer and the reader or audience.

gerund A gerund is a noun derived from a verb ending in *-ing. Knitting is a relaxing and practical hobby.*

helping verb See *auxiliary verb.*

homonym Homonyms are words that sound alike but are spelled differently and have separate meanings. *They're waiting for their dinner to be served.*

idiomatic verb Idiomatic verbs require a specific preposition or prepositions to create a new meaning from the same base verb. These verbs are also called two-word or phrasal verbs. This class of verbs also includes those whose accompanying prepositions are less predictable. *She got over her illness quickly.* See Part 8, Prepositions, p. 141, for more examples of phrasal verbs and their particles.

imperative mood The imperative mood is used to give commands, make requests, and issue instructions. *Wash your hands before preparing food.*

indefinite article The indefinite article *a/an* is a kind of determiner that is used when the identity of the noun modified is not expected to be known to the reader, such as when a noun is introduced for the first time. *An* is a variant of *a* that goes directly before a word beginning with a vowel sound. *A strange man walked up to me on the street at night chewing an apple.*

independent clause An independent clause is one that contains a complete thought and can stand alone as a simple sentence.

indicative mood The indicative mood expresses statements of fact. Most kinds of speaking and writing are in the indicative mood. All three sentences in this entry are in the indicative mood, as are most of the sentences in this workbook.

indirect object An indirect object is a noun, noun phrase, or pronoun that follows a transitive verb and tells for whom/what or to whom/what the action is done. *Throw me the ball.*

infinitive The infinitive is the base form of the verb + *to*. You can use the infinitive in particular verbal phrases to state intentions, desires, or expectations. *I wanted to watch the homecoming parade from the balcony.*

informal speech/writing Informal speech and writing are conversational and colloquial. For example, a telephone conversation with a relative, an e-mail message sent to a friend, or a chat with the person sitting next to you on the bus will most likely be informal. This type of speech and writing bends—or sometimes entirely ignores—some of the grammar rules of English in order to create a kind of verbal shorthand: *Can't do much about it now* (explicit subject is missing). Generally, informal speech and writing feature shorter words rather than longer ones, and idiomatic expressions and slang are common.

intensive pronoun Intensive pronouns are created by adding *-self* or *-selves* to personal pronouns: *myself, yourself, himself, herself, itself, ourselves, yourselves,* and *themselves.* Intensive pronouns emphasize their antecedent. *I crocheted this sweater myself.*

intransitive verb An intransitive verb expresses action that is not directed toward a direct object. Such verbs are often followed by an adverb. *They dressed quickly.*

modal Modals are auxiliary verbs used most often in making requests and giving instructions. The nine most common modals are the pairs *can/could, will/would, shall/should, may/might,* and *must* (which has no pair). *Would you proofread my paper, please?*

modifier The word *modifier* comes from the verb *modify,* which means "to change in some way." Modifiers change the words they modify by describing them, limiting them, or making them more specific. *The chair,* for example, becomes *the green chair.* Even more specific would be *the green folding chair.*

mood Mood refers to how the speaker or writer intends a statement to be understood: as a fact (the indicative mood), as a command (the imperative mood), or as a desire, suggestion, or improbability (the subjunctive mood).

noncount noun A noncount noun names an item that is difficult or impossible to count. It does not have a plural. *Pour me a glass of milk, please.*

noun A noun is a word that names a person (*cousin*), place (*supermarket*), thing (*eraser*), or concept (*forgiveness*). Proper nouns name specific people, places, things, or concepts (*Oklahoma*). Collective nouns name groups (*team*). Nouns that have both singular and plural forms are called count nouns. Noncount nouns do not have a plural form.

noun clause A noun clause is a clause that functions as a noun within a sentence. You can use noun clauses to combine two sentences into one, with one sentence functioning as the independent clause and the other as a dependent clause embedded within the main sentence. *That I spoke Spanish proved to be very useful.*

object pronoun Object pronouns function as the object of a sentence, clause, or phrase. The object pronouns are *me, us, you, him, her, it, them, whom,* and *whomever. We bought them opera tickets.*

participle Participles are adjectives that have been created from verbs by adding suffixes, usually *-ed* and *-ing.* The **present participle** describes the thing or person causing the feeling or action. *The terrifying roller coaster ride made the girl fear for her life.* The **past participle** describes the person having the feeling or experiencing the action. *The terrified girl held on to the side of the roller coaster for dear life.*

phrasal verb See *idiomatic verb.*

phrasal-prepositional verb Phrasal-prepositional verbs are idiomatic verbs that combine *verb + adverbial particle + prepositional* sequence to create sentences such as *He just gave up on finishing his degree.*

phrase A phrase is a group of words expressing a coherent thought that does not include both a subject and a finite verb. Noun phrase: *A beautiful day.* Prepositional phrase: *To the museum.*

plural The form of a noun, verb, or pronoun that refers to more than one of something.

possessive pronoun Possessive pronouns show possession or ownership. The possessive pronouns are *my/mine, our/ours, your/your, his, her/hers, its, their/theirs,* and *whose/whosever. Her singing was beautiful.*

predicate A predicate is the part of a sentence that tells what the subject does. It consists of a verb and all its auxiliaries, modifiers, and complements.

predicate adjective A predicate adjective is an adjective that is separated from the noun it describes by a linking verb or another verb that functions similarly. *Something is wrong with the stove.*

preposition Prepositions are words that show the relationship between other words. Some of the most common prepositions are *in, on, at, to, from, by, for, of,* and *with.*

prepositional phrase A prepositional phrase is made up of a preposition followed by a noun or pronoun. *We took a cab from the restaurant to the theater.*

prepositional verb A prepositional verb is an idiomatic verb that requires a specific preposition or prepositions to be complete; it cannot stand alone without its proper preposition. *Wearing baggy pants is a fashion that caught on in the 90s.*

pronoun A pronoun is a word that takes the place of a noun, another pronoun, or a phrase functioning as a noun. You can use pronouns to avoid repeating previously mentioned words. The word or group of words replaced by the pronoun is called the **antecedent**. Usually pronouns occur after the antecedent has already been stated, although they may also occur before the antecedent. Pronouns must agree with their antecedents in case, number, and gender.

reflexive pronoun A reflexive pronoun is created by adding *-self* or *-selves* to a personal pronoun: *myself, yourself, himself, herself, itself, ourselves, yourselves,* and *themselves.* Reflexive pronouns occur in the object position when the subject and object are the same. *Overcome with guilt, the criminal turned himself in.*

relative pronoun Relative pronouns link dependent clauses to independent clauses to form complete sentences from two separate ideas. The relative pronouns are *who, whom, whose, which,* and *that. The new supervisor, who has just started work this week, is feeling overwhelmed by the challenges of his new position.*

sentence A sentence is an independent clause punctuated as an individual unit. *He won $2,000 on a television game show.*

simple sentence A simple sentence is the most basic sentence in English, containing just a subject and a predicate. *She waved.*

singular The form of a noun, verb, or pronoun that refers to just one of something.

subject pronoun Subject pronouns function as the subject of a sentence or clause. The subject pronouns are *I, we, you, he, she, it, they, who,* and *whoever. They were going to the opera that evening.*

subject-verb-object word order The subject-verb-object word order is the most common in contemporary English statements. *She has a pet rabbit.* Questions in English are an exception: they place a verb before the subject. *Does she have a pet rabbit?*

subjunctive mood The subjunctive mood in English expresses a desire, suggestion, or improbability. The subjunctive is indicated by the form of the verb. *My mother asked that I call her when my plane lands.*

subordinating conjunction A subordinating conjunction introduces an adverb clause and indicates the relationship between the adverb clause and another clause (generally, an independent clause). *I liked dried pasta until I tasted fresh, homemade noodles.*

superlative form The superlative form is an adjective or adverb used in making comparisons among three or more things. Superlative adjectives usually end in *-est. That's the smartest cat I've ever seen.* Superlative adverbs are often formed from adjectives by adding the modifier *most* before the adjective. *He performed his work the most diligently of them all.*

tense Tense is the quality of a verb that indicates the time of action (or state of being) and type of action (or state of being). You can express tense through verb endings and auxiliary (helping) verbs. *She goes to the gym every day. She went to the gym yesterday. She had gone to the gym by the time I arrived home today. She will have been going to the gym for three consecutive months this Saturday.*

transitive verb A transitive verb expresses action directed toward a noun or pronoun (the direct object). *I read the book.*

two-word verb See *idiomatic verb.*

verb A verb is a word that shows action or a state of being. Verbs are used to join the subject to the rest of the sentence. *The boy ran across the street.*

voice, active and passive When referring to verbs, voice indicates whether the subject is acting (active voice) or being acted upon (passive voice). Active voice focuses on the agent responsible for the action in the sentence. Passive voice indicates that the acting agent is unknown or not of great importance in the context of the sentence. Passive voice can also be used deliberately to hide the agent responsible for the action. Active voice: *He wrote this book.* Passive voice: *This book was written by him.*

zero article The term *zero article* indicates the nonexistence of an article or a determiner in front of a noun. Zero article occurs only with noncount or plural count forms to signify general categories. *I'm afraid of snakes.* (There is no article or determiner in front of *snakes.*)

Appendix B
A Conjugated Verb

Conjugation of the Verb *Work*

Base form: work
Infinitive: to work

Present Tense

		Singular	Plural
First person		I work	we work
Second person		you work	you work
Third person	*masculine*	he works	they work
	feminine	she works	
	neuter	it works	

Past Tense

		Singular	Plural
First person		I worked	we worked
Second person		you worked	you worked
Third person	*masculine*	he worked	they worked
	feminine	she worked	
	neuter	it worked	

Future Tense

		Singular	Plural
First person		I will work	we will work
Second person		you will work	you will work
Third person	*masculine*	he will work	they will work
	feminine	she will work	
	neuter	it will work	

Present Progressive

		Singular	Plural
First person		I am working	we are working
Second person		you are working	you are working
Third person	*masculine*	he is working	they are working
	feminine	she is working	
	neuter	it is working	

Past Progressive

		Singular	Plural
First person		I was working	we were working
Second person		you were working	you were working
Third person	*masculine*	he was working	they were working
	feminine	she was working	
	neuter	it was working	

Future Progressive

		Singular	Plural
First person		I will be working	we will be working
Second person		you will be working	you will be working
Third person	*masculine*	he will be working	they will be working
	feminine	she will be working	
	neuter	it will be working	

Present Perfect

		Singular	Plural
First person		I have worked	we have worked
Second person		you have worked	you have worked
Third person	*masculine*	he has worked	they have worked
	feminine	she has worked	
	neuter	it has worked	

Past Perfect

		Singular	Plural
First person		I had worked	we had worked
Second person		you had worked	you had worked
Third person	*masculine*	he had worked	they had worked
	feminine	she had worked	
	neuter	it had worked	

Future Perfect

		Singular	Plural
First person		I will have worked	we will have worked
Second person		you will have worked	you will have worked
Third person	*masculine*	he will have worked	they will have worked
	feminine	she will have worked	
	neuter	it will have worked	

Present Perfect Progressive

		Singular	Plural
First person		I have been working	we have been working
Second person		you have been working	you have been working
Third person	*masculine*	he has been working	they have been working
	feminine	she has been working	
	neuter	it has been working	

Past Perfect Progressive

		Singular	Plural
First person		I had been working	we had been working
Second person		you had been working	you had been working
Third person	*masculine*	he had been working	they had been working
	feminine	she had been working	
	neuter	it had been working	

Future Perfect Progressive

		Singular	Plural
First person		I will have been working	we will have been working
Second person		you will have been working	you will have been working
Third person	*masculine*	he will have been working	they will have been working
	feminine	she will have been working	
	neuter	it will have been working	

Appendix C
Commonly Used Idiomatic Verbs

Be about to   be ready or prepared to do something; be on the verge of doing something

I am about to go to the grocery store; do you need anything there?

Be off   go away; leave

We have to load just one more bag and then we'll be off.

Be on to   find out about something or someone

My father was on to our plans to throw him a surprise party.

Catch on   to become popular; to understand something

You might feel lost at first, but you will soon catch on.

Caught on   past tense of *catch on*

The idea of cell phones caught on a long time ago.

Clear up   resolve or solve a problem; explain something previously misunderstood

We cleared up the misunderstanding quickly once we were able to talk in person.

Close down   not operate any longer; go out of business; also **shut down**

The clothing store closed down because it wasn't getting enough business.

Come across   find; discover

While going through her grandmother's closet, she came across a beautiful old fur coat.

Come back   return

I hope you'll come back soon.

Come up   be mentioned

If your name comes up during the meeting, I'll be sure to explain why you're not there.

Come up with   create; think of

Our brainstorming session helped us come up with some great ideas.

Dress up   wear nice, formal clothing

Some people like to dress up when they go to an expensive restaurant.

Drop in   (sometimes **drop by**) visit for a brief period of time, sometimes unexpectedly

He just dropped in to discuss the progress we've made on his project.

End up   become; conclude; finish (a certain result is usually specified). See also **turn out**.

The company ended up bankrupt because of unethical business practices.

Figure out determine or understand something; solve a problem

She couldn't figure out what he was trying to say.

Get away with escape with no punishment

He'll never get away with his crimes.

Get over recover

I hope he gets over his pneumonia soon.

Get (something) out of receive a benefit or profit from something in some way

Stockholders hope to get something out of their financial investments.

Get through survive; endure

We did our best to get through the tragedy.

Go along with agree with or participate in something

I'm not going along with his pranks anymore.

Hang around be someplace or near someplace (or someone)

The boys were hanging around the kitchen hoping dinner would be ready soon.

Hang on wait

Hang on, and I'll help you when I've finished washing the dishes.

Hang out spend time somewhere or with someone

We always hang out at the lake after school.

Hang with keep listening; keep paying attention to what someone is saying. See also **stick with**.

Are you hanging with me?

Laid out established

The company laid out its policy on tardiness.

Look forward to anticipate

I look forward to seeing you soon.

Make out understand

There was so much interference on the cell phone that I couldn't make out what my friend was saying.

Make up create; invent; lie

We need to make up some guidelines for using the photocopier.

Make up for compensate or atone for something

I made my husband chocolate chip cookies to make up for dropping his birthday cake.

Put off delay doing something; offend or annoy someone

I put off doing my homework too long, and now I have to stay up late to finish it.

He was put off by her casual attitude about their collaborative project.

Put on dress oneself in something (article of clothing)

I put on my hat, coat, and gloves and went outside.

Put up with   endure; tolerate

I'm not putting up with your silliness any longer.

Run into   meet unexpectedly

I ran into my neighbor while shopping at the mall.

Set out   leave (for a particular destination)

The fishermen set out early the next morning.

Slip up   make a mistake

I'm afraid I might slip up and say the wrong thing to him.

Start over   do something again from the beginning

When his building plans were not approved by the city, the contractor had to start over.

Stick with   (sometimes **hang with**) persevere with something or someone; continue doing something or continue being with someone

Just stick with your English studies, and little by little it will get easier.

Take after   resemble; look like

She takes after her mother more than her father.

Take down   transcribe something dictated; write something on paper; take notes

Take down this address, please.

Take off   depart; leave; remove

The plane took off.

Please take off your hat indoors.

Take on   accept

My sister always takes on more than she can possibly do.

Think back to   remember; recall

When I think back to my younger days, I wonder where all that youthful energy went!

Throw up   vomit. This expression is considered more polite than saying *vomit*.

After drinking too much milk, the baby threw up.

Tried out   made a trial of; experimented with; tried something for a period of time

He tried out that new restaurant but found the food too spicy for his taste.

Turn off   give a negative impression; annoy

The unprofessional behavior of the sales associate turned the customer off.

Turn out   conclude; finish (a certain result is usually specified). See also **end up**.

The high school musical turned out very well.

Wake up   awaken; stop sleeping

I wake up every morning at 7 A.M.

Appendix D
ESL Resources Online

Bedford/St. Martin's offers an extensive collection of grammar and writing exercises on the Exercise Central Web site: bedfordstmartins.com/exercisecentral/

In addition, the *Re:Writing* Web site contains interactive exercises that target ESL trouble spots: bedfordstmartins.com/rewriting

Additional ESL resources may also be found on the Web at the addresses listed below.

General

ESLPod: English for Everyone
http://www.eslpod.com

Purdue Online Writing Lab—ESL Resources
http://owl.english.purdue.edu/handouts/esl/index.html

ESL Blue(s)
http://www.collegeem.qc.ca/cemdept/anglais/

English Language Center Study Zone from the University of Victoria
http://web2.uvcs.uvic.ca/elc/studyzone/grammar.htm

Grammar Bytes!
http://www.chompchomp.com/

Guide to Grammar and Writing by the Capital Community College Foundation
http://cctc.commnet.edu/grammar/

Quizzes, Games, and Other Interactive Resources

Vocabulary and Grammar Activities for ESL Students
http://a4esl.org/

Hangman, Crossword Puzzles, and More
http://www.1-language.com/

ESL Games
http://www.manythings.org/

Grammar Exercises
http://www.eslgold.com

Discussion Boards

Dave's ESL Café
http://www.eslcafe.com/

EnglishForums.com
http://www.englishforums.com

Reference Tools

Babelfish Translation
http://babelfish.altavista.com/

Merriam-Webster Online
http://www.m-w.com/

Appendix E
Answers to Exercise Items

Part 1 Nouns

EXERCISE 1.1 Singular and Plural Nouns

1. immigrants **2.** ocean **3.** countries **4.** corners **5.** land **6.** ports **7.** tests **8.** diseases **9.** letters **10.** officials

EXERCISE 1.2 Singular and Plural Nouns

1. The Beatles were one of the most popular musical **acts** of all time. **2.** Four young **men** from Liverpool, England, made a fortune playing songs that young people loved. **3.** Recordings by the Beatles still sell millions of **copies** today. **4.** Some buyers are middle-aged fans who have not lost **respect** for the group. **5.** They may buy CDs since they no longer own stereo **equipment** that can play their old vinyl records. **6.** Playing **music** from their youth makes some fans feel young again. **7.** Other people who buy Beatles records are **teenagers** discovering the songs for the first time. **8.** Even today, a teenager is likely to know bits of Beatle **trivia**. **9.** Some young listeners become fans, but others don't understand the **fuss** about the Beatles. **10.** The two surviving Beatles are in their early sixties, but their fans span all **ages**.

EXERCISE 1.3 Singular and Plural Nouns

1. agency **2.** attempts **3.** role **4.** riders **5.** colonists **6.** president **7.** employees **8.** country **9.** train **10.** times

EXERCISE 1.4 Count and Noncount Nouns

1. number **2.** reasons **3.** immigrants **4.** wealth **5.** Overpopulation **6.** discrimination **7.** battles **8.** Legislation **9.** benefits **10.** advice

EXERCISE 1.5 Count and Noncount Nouns

1. According to a recent survey by the National Marriage Project, many young people in the United States believe that they will find one special person to offer them true **love**. **2.** The idea that every person has a soul mate can build dangerously high **expectations**. **3.** When people expect perfect romances, they may end **relationships** that are imperfect. **4.** Young adults need to be realistic when they think about the **qualities** they want in a life partner. **5.** Many **marriages** end because the partners have unrealistic ideas about married life. **6.** A potential partner's **suitability** as a parent did not matter much to most people who took the survey. **7.** Only 16 **percent** of the young adults surveyed believed that the main purpose of marriage was to have children. **8.** The idea that a couple should have common beliefs about **religion** was also viewed as unimportant. **9.** Is the United States becoming a nation of young **romantics**? **10.** Perhaps too many young people are getting their **information** about marriage from television and romance novels instead of from real-life examples.

EXERCISE 1.6 Count and Noncount Nouns

Hawaii is a chain of **(1.) islands** in the Pacific Ocean. The warm **(2.) weather** brings visitors from all over the world. The abundance of **(3.) fruit** is also an attraction; there's nothing like eating a fresh **(4.) pineapple** for breakfast. Another attraction is the natural beauty of Hawaii's geographical **(5.) features** such as volcanoes, waterfalls, and beaches. Enjoying the natural beauty is a great way to find **(6.) relief** from a hectic lifestyle. Hawaii also has many natural **(7.) resources**. One of them is **(8.) coffee**. Visitors will also find many spas promoting **(9.) relaxation**. Certainly, Hawaii has inspired many **(10.) people** to visit again.

Part 2 Articles

EXERCISE 2.1 Articles

1. A **2.** the **3.** X **4.** a **5.** the **6.** a **7.** X **8.** A **9.** an **10.** an

EXERCISE 2.2 Articles

1. The U.S. Constitution guarantees freedom of religion to all residents of the country. **2.** Correct **3.** Instead, by law, all residents are allowed to worship as they please or to choose not to worship at all. **4.** The U.S. Supreme Court declared school prayer unconstitutional about forty years ago. **5.** Correct **6.** Correct **7.** Student religious organizations can meet before school starts. **8.** However, teachers or other authority figures in a school may not legally lead prayers in class or at school functions. **9.** The U.S. Constitution does not restrict the practice of personal religious beliefs. **10.** But, the law does not permit the use of class time in public schools for group expression of a particular faith.

EXERCISE 2.3 Articles

1. Politicians in most [**no article necessary**] states now realize the importance of trying to win the Hispanic vote. **2.** Grouping all Hispanics together ignores **the** fact that Hispanic Americans come from many different countries and cultures. **3. The** cultures of Cuba and Mexico are different, just as the cultures of France and Sweden are different. **4.** Just as not all Irish Americans agree on political issues, there is not **a** single issue that guarantees all Hispanics' approval. **5.** Some issues may capture **the** interest of the majority of Hispanic American voters, however. **6.** A high percentage of Hispanic residents of the United States believe that the government should provide assistance to **the** poor. **7.** Government help to reduce poverty is usually considered **a** liberal position. **8.** However, many Hispanic Americans are in [**no article necessary**] agreement with conservative political opinions about social issues. **9.** In 2001, George W. Bush became **the** first U.S. president to broadcast a speech in Spanish to appeal to Hispanic American voters. **10.** His tactic may or may not have had **an** effect on Hispanic approval of his positions, for Hispanics in this country also disagree about the politics of speaking Spanish.

EXERCISE 2.4 Articles

1. the **2.** a **3.** the **4.** the **5.** A **6.** A **7.** a **8.** an **9.** a **10.** a

Part 3 Pronouns

EXERCISE 3.1 Personal Pronouns

1. I **2.** They **3.** We **4.** He **5.** I **6.** I **7.** He **8.** we **9.** we **10.** I

EXERCISE 3.2 Personal Pronouns

1. you **2.** You **3.** they **4.** they **5.** they **6.** you **7.** We **8.** I **9.** they **10.** They

EXERCISE 3.3 Personal Pronouns

1. pronoun: he; antecedent: Mahatma Gandhi **2.** pronoun: he; antecedent: Mahatma Gandhi **3.** pronoun: he; antecedent: he **4.** pronoun: he; antecedent: Gandhi **5.** pronoun: I; antecedent: father **6.** pronoun: we; antecedent: us **7.** pronoun: I; antecedent: me **8.** pronoun: I; antecedent: I **9.** pronoun: he; antecedent: Gandhi **10.** pronoun: He; antecedent: Gandhi

EXERCISE 3.4 Personal Pronouns

1. It 2. They 3. it 4. they 5. We 6. I 7. they 8. it 9. she 10. he

EXERCISE 3.5 Personal Pronouns

1. You 2. They 3. He 4. He 5. She 6. they 7. you 8. I 9. It 10. they

EXERCISE 3.6 Personal Pronouns

1. pronoun: I; antecedent: me 2. pronoun: She; antecedent: her cousin 3. pronoun: he; antecedent: band leader 4. pronoun: we; antecedent: us 5. pronoun: he; antecedent: drummer 6. pronoun: they; antecedent: band 7. pronoun: she; antecedent: cousin 8. pronoun: he; antecedent: groom 9. pronoun: he; antecedent: groom 10. pronoun: they; antecedent: band

EXERCISE 3.7 Object Pronouns

1. him 2. it 3. her 4. him 5. her 6. it 7. him 8. it 9. him 10. them

EXERCISE 3.8 Object Pronouns

1. them 2. her 3. him 4. her 5. them 6. it 7. you 8. me 9. me 10. them

EXERCISE 3.9 Object Pronouns

1. me 2. them 3. it 4. me 5. me; it 6. me; him 7. It 8. her 9. me 10. it

EXERCISE 3.10 Possessive Pronouns

1. his 2. his 3. her 4. her 5. his 6. its; his 7. his 8. their 9. their 10. our

EXERCISE 3.11 Possessive Pronouns

1. his; his 2. their 3. her 4. his 5. his 6. her 7. her 8. their 9. his 10. its

EXERCISE 3.12 Possessive Pronouns

1. my 2. our 3. her 4. his 5. our 6. my 7. my 8. my 9. their 10. my

EXERCISE 3.13 Object/Possessive Pronouns

1. its 2. Your 3. them 4. them; their 5. it 6. their 7. their 8. their 9. your; them 10. their; you

EXERCISE 3.14 Object/Possessive Pronouns

1. their 2. their 3. my 4. their; them 5. me 6. his 7. me 8. my 9. it 10. your

EXERCISE 3.15 Object/Possessive Pronouns

1. their 2. them 3. his 4. her; her 5. them 6. us 7. their 8. me; them 9. her 10. his

EXERCISE 3.16 Object/Possessive Pronouns

1. their 2. their 3. him 4. her 5. them 6. his 7. your 8. you 9. your 10. them 11. their

EXERCISE 3.17 Reflexive/Intensive Pronouns

1. yourself 2. themselves 3. yourself 4. himself 5. ourselves 6. herself 7. myself 8. ourselves 9. himself 10. ourselves

EXERCISE 3.18 Reflexive/Intensive Pronouns

1. herself 2. himself 3. herself 4. themselves 5. himself 6. yourself 7. myself 8. himself 9. ourselves 10. yourselves

EXERCISE 3.19 Reflexive/Intensive Pronouns

1. themselves 2. himself 3. herself 4. themselves 5. myself 6. himself 7. ourselves 8. yourself 9. herself 10. myself

EXERCISE 3.20 Reflexive/Intensive Pronouns

1. themselves 2. myself 3. herself 4. ourselves 5. themselves 6. himself 7. herself 8. myself 9. oneself 10. myself

EXERCISE 3.21 Reflexive/Intensive Pronouns

1. myself 2. herself 3. themselves 4. herself 5. himself 6. ourselves 7. themselves 8. herself 9. himself 10. myself

EXERCISE 3.22 Reflexive/Intensive Pronouns

1. himself 2. themselves 3. yourself 4. herself 5. ourselves 6. myself 7. herself 8. themselves 9. himself 10. ourselves

EXERCISE 3.23 Relative Pronouns

1. whom 2. whom 3. that 4. that 5. which 6. that 7. which 8. which 9. that 10. whom

EXERCISE 3.24 Relative Pronouns

1. which 2. whom 3. that 4. that 5. whom 6. that 7. which 8. that 9. whom 10. that (for answers 2, 5, and 9 *who* would also be correct in informal situations)

EXERCISE 3.25 Relative Pronouns

Possible Answers 1. The Taj Mahal is a monument **that** is considered one of the most beautiful sites in the world. **2.** The Taj Mahal is a memorial **that** King Shah Jahan built for his queen, Mumtaz Mahal. **3.** It is also an ancient mausoleum **that** holds the tomb of Mumtaz Mahal. **4.** King Shah Jahan wanted to show his deep love for Mumtaz Mahal, **who** died during childbirth. **5.** The King decreed that the Taj Mahal be built in a special location **that** had to be both scenic and close to his palace. **6.** The King wanted to build a monument **that** no one would ever forget. **7.** Shah Jahan selected skilled architects and masons **who** came from all over India and the Middle East. **8.** The Taj Mahal is made of marble, precious stones, and gems, **which** made it a very expensive project. **9.** Every year, the Taj Mahal attracts millions of visitors **who** are always surprised at the grandeur and size of the monument. **10.** The Taj Mahal is an extraordinary monument **that** is a testimony to the deep love Shah Jahan had for his wife.

Part 4 Negative Statements and Questions

EXERCISE 4.1 Negative Statements

1. In my first year of college, most of my friends **did not choose** to study one of the romance languages. **2.** More recently, languages such as Chinese or Japanese **have not been** more popular. **3.** Studying a new language in the early morning **has not been** satisfying. **4.** I **did not learn** several thousand kanji characters. **5.** Learning the kanji characters also **did not help** me learn Japanese. **6.** The Japanese language **does not use** kanji characters in its written language. **7.** I **did not practice** speaking Chinese with native speakers at my college. **8.** They **did not say** that they understood me. **9.** I **do not believe** they were telling me the truth. **10.** I **did not love** learning and speaking another language.

EXERCISE 4.2 Negative Statements

1. Political scandals **have not filled** U.S. history in the past thirty years. **2.** Politicians **have not been caught** stealing, lying, and cheating. **3.** President Richard Nixon **did not leave** the Presidential office after Watergate. **4.** Many political scandals **do not have** "-gate" in their name because of Watergate. **5.** Some politicians **have not been accused** of being involved with crime groups. **6.** Sometimes, the public **does not demand** resignation. **7.** The politician **might not admit** his wrongdoing. **8.** Other times, politicians **do not defend** themselves against accusations. **9.** Some politicians **do not confess** publicly. **10.** Because of scandals, the public **does not find** it difficult to trust politicians.

EXERCISE 4.3 Negative Statements

1. Before the invention of the modern airplane, people **did not travel** by car or railway. **2.** People **did not own** only one car for road trips. **3.** Better highways **were not constructed** as more and more people traveled by car. **4.** The railway **did not provide** an alternate mode of traveling. **5.** Railway trains **did not offer** luxury accommodations such as sleeping cabins and fine restaurants. **6.** People also **did not find** a way to travel overseas: luxury cruise ships. **7.** Cruise ship operators **did not take** into account the length of the journey in their plans. **8.** Airlines also **did not begin** offering luxury accommodations such as first class seats and hot meals on flights. **9.** Some airlines even **did not have** fully reclining seats and televisions for each passenger. **10.** Perhaps one day there **will not be** gyms on airplanes!

EXERCISE 4.4 Negative Statements

1. Van Gogh **did not learn** to paint as a young man. **2.** His paintings **cannot be** seen in museums around the world. **3.** He **is not best known** for his textured brush strokes. **4.** He **did not paint** with oil paints to produce rich scenes of nature. **5.** Van Gogh w**as not close** to his brother, Theo. **6.** He **did not suffer** from depression and an addiction to absinthe. **7.** Those two afflictions **did not make** his paintings more intense. **8.** He **did not die** just around the time his artwork was becoming famous. **9.** Many collectors and museums **have not bought** his paintings. **10.** Van Gogh's famous painting of sunflowers **did not sell** for millions of dollars.

EXERCISE 4.5 Questions

1. Were the Beatles from Liverpool, England? **2.** Were there four musicians in the band? **3.** Did Paul McCartney and John Lennon write many of the songs? **4.** Was the band's first successful single "Love Me Do"? **5.** Is the term for the crazed obsession with the Beatles called "Beatlemania"? **6.** Did the band perform on the *Ed Sullivan Show* in the United States in February 1964? **7.** Did they also star in the movie *A Hard Day's Night*? **8.** Was John Lennon's wife's name Yoko Ono? **9.** Was the band's last performance in San Francisco? **10.** Did the band officially break up in 1970?

EXERCISE 4.6 Questions

1. Did your cousin graduate from law school on Saturday? **2.** Is his area of concentration business law? **3.** Was his undergraduate degree in history? **4.** Did he choose history because it seemed like a good pre-law degree? **5.** Were there 150 students who graduated with him? **6.** Is the law school located in southern Florida? **7.** Does he plan to take the bar exam in July? **8.** Would he like to move to Washington, D.C.? **9.** Does he plan to move with his best friend? **10.** Does he want to live in Washington, D.C., because it has so many opportunities?

EXERCISE 4.7 Questions

Possible Answers 1. When does the summer Olympics take place? **2.** What sporting events does the Olympics feature? **3.** Who competes in the events, and what do they compete for? **4.** Where did the summer Olympics of 2004 take place? **5.** When did the first modern Olympic Games take place? **6.** What is the decathlon? **7.** How long is the marathon? **8.** Why did the United States boycott the Olympics in 1980? **9.** Why did the Soviet Union boycott the Olympics in 1984? **10.** What do the five rings on the Olympic flag represent?

EXERCISE 4.8 Questions

Possible Answers 1. What is the awards ceremony for the motion picture industry called? **2.** Why was the awards ceremony created? **3.** Where does the ceremony take place? **4.** When does the ceremony usually take place? **5.** Who sees the ceremony on TV? **6.** What do celebrities wear to the ceremony? **7.** What are the most popular categories? **8.** Which film won ten awards in 2004? **9.** Who won the award for best actor in 2005? **10.** When will the 78th Academy Awards take place?

Part 5 Sentences and Clauses

EXERCISE 5.1 Sentence Subjects

1. X **2.** It **3.** it **4.** it **5.** There **6.** it **7.** X **8.** There **9.** it **10.** there

EXERCISE 5.2 Word Order in Sentences

1. Many people **believe** that too much sex and violence is shown on television. **2.** Most parents would **like** to monitor their children's television viewing. **3.** For many people, however, keeping track of a child's choice of television programs **is** impossible. **4.** One solution might **come** from recent technological innovations. **5.** Several years ago, American television manufacturers **agreed** to start equipping all new televisions with a V-chip. **6.** The V **stands** for "violence." **7.** The V-chip **screens** out shows that contain sex and violence. **8.** Parents **program** the chip to block shows with certain ratings. **9.** With the V-chip, individuals, not the government, **censor** their children's television programs. **10.** Of course, today, many children **know** better than their parents how to program electronic devices.

EXERCISE 5.3 Word Order in Sentences

Possible Answers 1. The television industry provides ratings for television programs so that parents can decide what to allow their children to watch. **2.** The ratings system is similar to the one used for movies. **3.** The ratings system exists already, but people get a V-chip only when they buy a new television. **4.** Older children might be attracted to programming rated as explicit. **5.** Most parents know that kids want what they are not allowed to have. **6.** Parents with an older television will not be able to block out shows rated for mature audiences. **7.** Some critics say that it is only a matter of time before a child learns to tamper with the V-chip programmer. **8.** Advertisers worry that parents will block out the prime-time shows that generate the most advertising revenue. **9.** If a show has an explicit rating, parents might block it out and advertisers might shy away. **10.** The television industry argues that the V-chip is a kind of censorship since it will indirectly control the kinds of shows produced.

EXERCISE 5.4 Noun Clauses

1. Many companies sending executives abroad believe <u>that their most difficult challenge will be helping their employees deal with culture shock in a foreign environment</u>. **object clause 2.** <u>How companies can help executives to cope when they return</u> is an even more serious problem. **subject clause 3.** Recent research proves <u>that these professionals are unsatisfied with the way their companies are handling their repatriation</u>. **object clause 4.** A study reveals <u>that 25 percent of returning employees leave their companies within a year</u>. **object clause 5.** <u>Whatever investment the company made in the employee</u> is lost when the employee leaves. **subject clause 6.** <u>That so much money is at stake</u> motivates top managers to investigate the reasons for employee dissatisfaction. **subject clause 7.** Many people wonder <u>whether much employee dissatisfaction stems from poor planning by the company</u>. **object clause 8.** Many returning executives complain <u>that their companies didn't tell them exactly what they would be working on when they returned</u>. **object clause 9.** A majority of returnees are unable to use the experience they gained abroad, which demonstrates <u>that companies are not thinking ahead</u>. **object clause 10.** <u>How companies will address these repatriation issues</u> is a challenge for today's business world. **subject clause**

EXERCISE 5.5 Noun Clauses

Possible Answers 1. The airline industry rarely discusses why passengers can only bring two pieces of luggage into the airplane cabin. **2.** It is mandatory that these two pieces not exceed certain size requirements. **3.** It was often the case that travelers couldn't fit everything they needed for a business trip into these small bags. **4.** Travelers had to hand over as checked luggage whichever bags exceeded size restrictions. **5.** It irritated many passengers that the airlines often lost checked baggage. **6.** In addition, it often interferes with busy travelers' schedules that checked bags take a long time to arrive at the baggage claim. **7.** It is encouraging that the airlines have been looking for solutions to this problem. **8.** Major airlines have suggested that airplanes should increase the amount of space available in overhead bins so that passengers can bring more and larger carry-ons. **9.** Recent studies have shown that airplanes can achieve departure six to eight minutes faster with the larger bins. **10.** It is uncertain whether flight attendants will be happy about this change.

EXERCISE 5.6 Noun Clauses

Possible Answers 1. It is evident why some companies are becoming concerned about what their employees are doing. **2.** Systems administrators can use software to see the amount of e-mail that employees send and receive each day. **3.** Is it necessary for the company to know that an employee e-mails jokes from a business computer? **4.** It could be considered a breach of privacy when managers read employees' e-mail. **5.** One employee said that she would sue her company for breach of privacy. **6.** The systems administrator tells employees that it is his job to prevent problems. **7.** There are many reasons that cause managers to install monitoring software. **8.** It is true that companies have to buy more bandwidth if their employees send huge amounts of e-mail. **9.** Lower-level employees are concerned whenever their e-mail is scrutinized but senior executives' e-mail is not. **10.** It is important that managers create an atmosphere that makes employees feel trusted and fairly treated.

EXERCISE 5.7 Adjective Clauses

Possible Answers 1. I spoke to a surgeon who said that plastic surgery is sometimes a parent's idea rather than a teen's. **2.** However, more often the teenager is the one who convinces the parent to pay for procedures. **3.** High school can be a harsh environment in which the slightest physical imperfections can provoke torment and teasing. **4.** Media images of young men and women to which teens are frequently exposed show impossibly perfect faces and bodies. OR Teens are frequently exposed to media images of young men and women that show impossibly perfect faces and bodies. **5.** Like it or not, we are living in a superficial culture in which attractive people get better treatment than unattractive people. **6.** Therefore, people whose bodies aren't even fully developed are requesting plastic surgery. **7.** One woman who was insistent about changing her appearance went to a plastic surgeon's office. **8.** She demanded to have the wrinkles that were around her eyes removed. **9.** There were just two problems, which the surgeon pointed out to her. **10.** The problems, which prevented her from having the surgery, were that she was nineteen years old and that she had no wrinkles. OR The problems, which were that she was nineteen years old and that she had no wrinkles, prevented her from having the surgery.

EXERCISE 5.8 Adjective Clauses

Possible Answers Nowadays, there are several Internet sites that [delete **they**] show live broadcasts of cosmetic surgery. If people miss the live coverage, they can pull up archival video footage in **which** patients undergo procedures from liposuction to facelifts. This new trend shows that plastic surgery has gone from something **that** was considered shameful or vain to something **that** is considered normal or even a status symbol. The ten million Americans who had plastic surgery in the 1990s represent every social stratum. Moreover, the majority of Americans **who** had plastic surgery came from households that [delete **they**] earned below $60,000. The popularity of the Web casts also demonstrates how much people love to watch live procedures **in** which there is a lot of blood and gore. How do patients feel about being the subject of broadcasts in **which** their bodies are sliced open? Apparently, just fine; the procedures, **which** are free for patients who model for Web casts, attract hundreds of emails per day from candidates.

EXERCISE 5.9 Conditional Sentences

1. had **2.** not watch **3.** were **4.** were **5.** would take **6.** are **7.** were **8.** turn **9.** isn't **10.** becomes

EXERCISE 5.10 Conditional Sentences

Possible Answers 1. wants **2.** receive (OR will receive) **3.** appear (OR will appear) **4.** want **5.** wanted **6.** would sell **7.** would start **8.** had believed **9.** does not plan **10.** would have filled out (OR would fill out) **11.** use **12.** are **13.** will think **14.** were **15.** do not have **16.** may end up

Part 6 Verbs

EXERCISE 6.1 Simple Present Tense

1. means **2.** knows **3.** swim **4.** occurs **5.** happen **6.** wish **7.** believe **8.** foretell **9.** take **10.** thank

EXERCISE 6.2 Simple Past Tense

1. crashed **2.** thought **3.** captured **4.** dared **5.** left **6.** knew **7.** came **8.** reached **9.** found **10.** discovered

EXERCISE 6.3 Present and Past Tenses

1. went **2.** remember **3.** became **4.** was **5.** have to **6.** repeated **7.** was **8.** graduated **9.** started **10.** take

EXERCISE 6.4 Present and Past Tenses

1. In 1995, my eighth-grade teacher told us we **had** to take our state's math and reading tests at the end of the school year. **2.** My teacher **spent** the whole spring of 1996 drilling us on the practice tests. **3.** School officials came to our class and announced that students **could not** pass or fail the test. **4.** Instead, they said that our school and the teachers **were** being tested. **5.** The students agreed that nobody **was** fooled by the officials' remarks. **6.** My friend Hector said, "The test results **are** going to be sent to our parents." **7.** In May of that year, we **sat** in class every day for a week completing the test. **8.** I **scored** in the fiftieth percentile, so my results were exactly average. **9.** Now I think of those results and **remember** the eighth grade fondly. **10.** I still believe that kids **learn** more in school when less time is spent on test preparation.

EXERCISE 6.5 Perfect Tenses

1. has been considering; present perfect **2.** will have spent; future perfect **3.** had served; past perfect **4.** will have provided; future perfect **5.** had hoped; past perfect **6.** has tried; present perfect **7.** has dreamed; present perfect **8.** had wanted; past perfect **9.** has assured; present perfect **10.** will have decided; future perfect

EXERCISE 6.6 Progressive Tenses

1. is moving **2.** was teaching **3.** was receiving **4.** was noticing **5.** is hoping **6.** were visiting **7.** are hunting **8.** will be looking **9.** are wishing **10.** is looking

EXERCISE 6.7 Modals

1. would **2.** can **3.** would **4.** can **5.** might **6.** should **7.** could **8.** would **9.** would; might **10.** Will

EXERCISE 6.8 Modals

1. I soon discovered that I **had to** choose a major after two years of coursework. **2.** I **couldn't** decide what career field interested me most, so selecting a major was difficult. **3.** At the beginning of my third year of coursework, I **had to** make a choice. **4.** My adviser told me that

I **could** change my mind later if I decided I wasn't happy with my decision. **5.** I decided that I **would** study engineering. **6.** When I took my first engineering course, I discovered that I **couldn't** understand some of the math required to complete my homework assignments. **7.** I realized that I **should** have taken more advanced math courses to prepare for my engineering classes. **8.** Now I am taking an extra math course to catch up, and I **should** finish my engineering degree next spring. **9.** I **couldn't** wait until I started work as an engineer. **10.** In the meantime, my professors tell me that I **should** study diligently to prepare for my career.

EXERCISE 6.9 Modals

Possible Answers 1. would have studied **2.** had to struggle **3.** would have considered (OR might have considered) **4.** would have stayed (OR might have stayed) **5.** had to venture (OR should venture) **6.** can enjoy (OR will enjoy) **7.** would have (OR might have) **8.** would feel (OR might feel) **9.** would miss (OR might miss) **10.** will prepare (OR can prepare)

EXERCISE 6.10 *To be* Verbs

1. is **2.** are **3.** is **4.** was **5.** were **6.** are **7.** were **8.** are **9.** am **10.** am

EXERCISE 6.11 *To be* Verbs

1. was **2.** were **3.** was **4.** be **5.** were **6.** is **7.** is **8.** am **9.** was **10.** is

EXERCISE 6.12 Verb Phrases

1. regarded **2.** learned **3.** face **4.** are trying **5.** asked **6.** involve **7.** volunteer **8.** believe **9.** achieve **10.** united

EXERCISE 6.13 Verb Phrases

Possible Answers 1. Students of English **are** often **surprised** by the differences between written and conversational English. **2.** Those students who **have studied** formal written English may find conversational English difficult to understand. **3.** Students who **have** recently **come** to an English-speaking country may have particular trouble with slang vocabulary and expressions. **4.** Conversation classes in English **are supposed** to help students become familiar with spoken English by simulating real-life situational dialogues. **5.** Students who **have** not **been exposed** to spoken English can listen to English radio or TV broadcasts to help them learn English. **6.** Just listening to spoken English **can be useful** in learning oral speech patterns and intonation. **7.** Many students find that listening to songs with English lyrics **can help** them learn new vocabulary and expressions. OR Many students find that listening to songs with English lyrics **helps** them learn new vocabulary and expressions. **8.** Some students who **do** not **feel** a need to learn spoken English might prefer to listen to radio broadcasts in their native language rather than broadcasts in English. **9.** If such students do not make a great effort to learn conversational English, they **may** never **understand** the spoken language well. **10.** Students in English classes who **may** not **have been working** hard on learning spoken English need to understand that an inability to speak and understand English can limit their opportunities.

EXERCISE 6.14 Simple, Perfect, and Progressive Verb Phrases

While I **was shopping** at a grocery store last week, I **counted** five different brands of bottled water on the shelves. These days, bottled water **costs** more than carbonated beverages, but many consumers now **feel** that good health is worth the greater price.

Nutrition experts **have observed** that Americans **consume** too much soda and junk food. Prior to these findings, some parents **noticed** that their children were more sluggish and inattentive after they **had eaten** junk food. In many cases, they **had been snacking** at school.

Now nutrition experts insist that children **need** breakfast before school so that they **do not stop** at vending machines for sodas or greasy snacks. Because studies **have shown** that students perform better when they eat nutritious foods, some schools **are considering** a ban on certain junk foods and soda machines. However, many parents **believe** that good nutrition should be enforced by parents, not schools. They **resent** being told by the school administration what not to put in their children's lunch. Based on recent sales of bottled water, it **appears** that consumers **are making** better nutritional choices.

EXERCISE 6.15 Simple, Perfect, and Progressive Verb Phrases

Possible Answers 1. Since then, the states **have** often **challenged** the federal government either by ignoring or refusing to implement the decision or by filing court cases. **2.** The case of Central High School in Little Rock, Arkansas, **is** one of the most famous examples of a state fighting this federal mandate. **3.** When the school **opened** in September 1957, the Arkansas National Guard was called out to prevent African Americans from entering the school. **4.** President Dwight D. Eisenhower ordered the army into Little Rock to enforce the court order, and African American children finally **entered** the school with the protection of federal troops. **5.** State-supported resistance to desegregation **did** not **end** with the Little Rock case. **6.** However, over the years the courts **have** consistently **ruled** in favor of desegregation. **7.** Racial integration of schools **remains** a concern for the current generation as well. **8.** Recent statistics **show** that about 35 percent of African American students go to schools in which 90 percent of the student body is nonwhite. **9.** In addition, support for integration **is declining** OR **has declined** in the current political climate. **10.** Today, the fight for desegregation **has been** largely **replaced** by the fight for quality education for all students.

EXERCISE 6.16 Participles

1. signaling **2.** cheering **3.** catching **4.** parading **5.** Smiling **6.** Carrying **7.** waving **8.** featuring **9.** marching **10.** rumbling

EXERCISE 6.17 Participles

1. Carrying **2.** growling **3.** noticing **4.** overflowing **5.** Wandering **6.** eating **7.** roaming **8.** picnicking **9.** looking **10.** finishing

EXERCISE 6.18 Participial Adjectives

1. excited **2.** soothing **3.** terrified **4.** tired **5.** observing **6.** shaking **7.** amazing **8.** horrifying **9.** satisfying **10.** surprised

EXERCISE 6.19 Participial Adjectives

1. Suffering patients have been used for medical students' practice in teaching hospitals for decades. **2.** Correct **3.** Sitting in a **packed** lecture hall, first- and second-year medical students can only imagine working on a real patient. **4.** However, **disgusted** patients soon tire of having amateurs use them to practice starting IVs, drawing blood, and giving injections. **5.** Correct **6.** Correct **7.** A **distressed** medical student may choke a mechanical patient repeatedly while trying to put a tube down its throat, and the machine will utter a loud gagging noise. **8.** The gagging sound is **unnerving**, but students' mistakes do not hurt any living human beings. **9.** The **uncomplaining** mechanical patients allow students to develop good medical techniques before they handle real people. **10.** When these teaching techniques become more widespread, hospitalized people all over the United States will be **relieved**.

EXERCISE 6.20 Infinitives and Gerunds

Since a university education in one country may differ from a university experience in another, students studying outside their native country may struggle **to understand** educational attitudes within foreign institutions. For example, in some countries students are expected **to avoid speaking** in class, but in other countries it is expected, if not required.

Moreover, instructors in some countries encourage students **to participate** actively by **solving** problems in groups, **making** presentations, and **examining** case studies.

Another aspect of the foreign classroom that is often confusing is the teacher-student relationship. In many countries this relationship is a formal one; in other countries it can appear **to be** more relaxed. Regardless of the level of formality between teacher and student, students should remember **to meet** deadlines for assignments and **to treat** the professor with respect. Even if a professor meets with students outside of class **to have** coffee with them, this shouldn't make the professor appear **to be** any less of an authority figure.

EXERCISE 6.21 Infinitives and Gerunds

1. to work **2.** to share **3.** to collaborate **4.** plagiarizing **5.** cheating **6.** to do **7.** to judge **8.** working **9.** asking **10.** angering

EXERCISE 6.22 Infinitives and Gerunds

1. International students who are considering **studying** in the United States should realize that relationships between students here can be either cooperative or competitive, depending on the class. **2.** International students who expect **to cooperate** with classmates may initially feel uncomfortable with the competition in American schools. **3.** Of course, they should not hesitate **to ask** their classmates for help. **4.** In some courses, however, the instructor might decide **to calculate** students' grades in relation to one another. **5.** This method of **grading** is called a curve. **6.** When a curve is used, students may be reluctant **to share** their lecture notes with others because they don't want to hurt their own grades. **7.** Students without high grade-point averages risk not **getting** into a top graduate program. **8.** Employers trying to fill a job opening may also choose **to look** at a candidate's grade-point average and faculty recommendations. **9.** When students under pressure are asked **to decide** between helping classmates and decreasing competition for a high grade-point average, they often choose the latter. **10.** International students sometimes have to get used to **functioning** in this competitive system.

Part 7 Modifiers

EXERCISE 7.1 Determiners

Historically, Japan has not been **a** country that encouraged immigration. **The** current labor shortage, however, may force **that** country to start allowing immigration. Because of **Japan's** low birthrate, not enough new workers are entering **the** workforce. Then, when women do have children, **few** new mothers stay in **the** job market. In addition, **Japan's** population is aging faster than **the** population of any other developed nation. Soon, **four** times as many Japanese citizens will be over age sixty-five as will be under **that** age. For **these three** reasons, **the** country will not be able to achieve economic growth or support itself unless it expands **its** labor pool. What strategy would have **a** more immediate effect than inviting immigration?

EXERCISE 7.2 Determiners

1. children's **2.** a **3.** many **4.** X **5.** a **6.** their **7.** Many **8.** a **9.** All **10.** this; America's

EXERCISE 7.3 Determiners

1. Many businesses today expect executives to be good public speakers. **2.** In fact, **a** person who cannot speak well in public is unlikely to be promoted to an executive position. **3.** However, 40 percent of all Americans have **a** terrible fear of public speaking. **4.** For these people, giving **a** speech is usually a miserable experience. **5.** Experts suggest a **few** ways to help conquer a fear of public speaking. **6.** Taking **a** few deep breaths before a speech gives the speaker extra oxygen and can calm nerves. **7.** Some speakers feel more confident when they imagine the audience in **their** underwear. **8.** When speakers remember something that made them laugh recently, **the** funny memory can help them to relax. **9.** People who have [**no determiner necessary**] extreme problems with public speaking might need professional help. **10.** Many organizations can help to conquer a **businessperson's** fear of giving speeches.

EXERCISE 7.4 Modifiers

1. a few **2.** a little **3.** any **4.** a few **5.** a little **6.** any **7.** any **8.** a few **9.** any **10.** a little

EXERCISE 7.5 Modifiers

1. a few **2.** a few **3.** a little **4.** any **5.** A little **6.** any **7.** a few **8.** any **9.** a few **10.** any

EXERCISE 7.6 Modifiers

1. Many **2.** many **3.** much **4.** Some **5.** many **6.** Some **7.** many **8.** much **9.** many **10.** much

EXERCISE 7.7 Modifiers

1. some **2.** any **3.** some **4.** any **5.** some **6.** some **7.** Some **8.** any **9.** any **10.** some

EXERCISE 7.8 Modifiers

1. this **2.** those **3.** this **4.** this **5.** these **6.** this **7.** that **8.** that **9.** these **10.** this

EXERCISE 7.9 Modifiers

1. this **2.** these **3.** those **4.** this **5.** that **6.** these **7.** those **8.** that **9.** that **10.** this

EXERCISE 7.10 Modifiers

1. This **2.** these **3.** this **4.** This **5.** these **6.** These **7.** this **8.** this **9.** these **10.** This

EXERCISE 7.11 Adjectives

1. <u>tattered</u> jersey **2.** <u>faded</u> number **3.** <u>school</u> mascot **4.** <u>all</u> students **5.** <u>basketball</u> game **6.** <u>final</u> game **7.** <u>shortest</u> member **8.** <u>star</u> player **9.** <u>unbelievable</u> shot **10.** <u>terrific</u> game

EXERCISE 7.12 Adjectives

1. <u>overstuffed</u> backpack **2.** <u>fashion</u> magazine **3.** <u>research</u> paper **4.** <u>dirty</u> look **5.** <u>rough</u> draft **6.** <u>unruly</u> mess; <u>old</u> sandwich **7.** <u>crumpled</u> draft **8.** <u>two</u> days **9.** <u>best</u> work **10.** <u>next</u> time

EXERCISE 7.13 Adjectives

Possible Answers 1. Most people with attention deficit disorder display **obvious** behavioral symptoms such as hyperactivity, disorganization, impulsiveness, and an inability to manage time effectively. **2. All** these symptoms affect performance in certain jobs. **3.** A.D.D. was once thought to exist only in a few **troublesome** children, but now experts believe that adults can also suffer from it. **4.** Nowadays, new research and openness about the condition help prevent **potential** job discrimination. **5.** Most adults would have trouble remaining completely focused on a **boring** thirty-minute slide presentation. **6.** For an adult with A.D.D., such a task is a **huge** cognitive burden. **7. Simple** modifications in the work routine can help A.D.D. sufferers to be more effective in their jobs. **8.** Organizing paperwork by color and size clears up **some** kinds of confusion for A.D.D. sufferers. **9.** For example, a **large** green folder might contain invoices, and a small blue folder could hold receipts. **10.** If it is not possible for them to change **confusing** daily office routines, A.D.D. sufferers should consider changing careers.

EXERCISE 7.14 Adjectives

The **black** crow called loudly from the shoulder of the **faded** scarecrow. The **neglected** garden had not been tended in years. Vegetables no longer grew in **neat** rows, because weeds and briars had taken their places. In **early** autumn, the house was put up for sale. One day, a car pulled into the driveway, and a **young** couple got out. They immediately loved the house and its garden. "This is perfect!" said the man to **his** wife, and she agreed. They bought the house and began to tend the **vegetable** garden at once. By summertime, the house was once again lovely, and vegetables were again growing in the **beautiful** garden.

EXERCISE 7.15 Adjectives

The origin of the roller coaster is an **interesting** one. **Early** roller coasters, in fact, did not roll at all. They were slides made from **hard** wood and then covered with **layered** sheets of ice. **Brave** riders would climb stairs leading up to the back of the slides. Once at the top, the passengers would rocket down the **frightening** 50 degree drop and then climb an **additional** set of stairs leading to the **next** slide. These **thrilling** slides were a favorite of Catherine the Great, and legend has it that she had **several** slides constructed on her estate to entertain guests.

EXERCISE 7.16 Adverbs

1. <u>slowly</u> turned 2. <u>eerily</u> creaked 3. <u>loudly</u> called 4. <u>finally</u> answered 5. <u>briskly</u> walking 6. <u>regularly</u> spent 7. <u>affectionately</u> known 8. <u>thoroughly</u> enjoyed 9. <u>suddenly</u> died 10. <u>especially</u> enjoyed

EXERCISE 7.17 Adverbs

Gus University is **extremely** proud of its men's track team, **especially** the star of the team, Andre. Andre runs very **fast**. In fact, he **recently** set a new record at Gus U for the 50 yard dash. **Today**, he is competing in the state meet. **Supposedly**, Olympic scouts are coming to watch him run. Coach Vasquez will be looking around **nervously**, trying to detect the scouts. **Fortunately**, Andre is more focused than his coach. **Calmly**, he will stretch his legs, arms, and body in preparation for his main event, the 50 yard dash. If Andre wins, he will **graciously** accept the handshakes of Coach Vasquez and me, the incognito Olympic scout.

EXERCISE 7.18 Adverbs

1. quickly 2. patiently 3. proudly 4. speedily 5. promptly 6. excitedly 7. knowingly 8. brightly 9. recently 10. wildly

EXERCISE 7.19 Adverbs

Traditionally, in this school district, Field Day is a competition among local high schools. Every year, students **eagerly** await it. Our coaches talk about team spirit and sportsmanship, but even so the events are **fiercely** competitive. They include track and field events as well as a tug of war. The events move **quickly**. Competitors **anxiously** wait for their scores. Murray High School has **consistently** won Field Day, so of course everyone wants to beat them. But this year might be their year to lose. A new event has **recently** been added: a poster contest. It means that even nonathletic students can **actively** participate in Field Day. The winning poster will be awarded 100 points. Who knows, maybe this year Murray High School can be stopped.

Part 8 Prepositions

EXERCISE 8.1 Prepositions

1. X 2. of 3. with 4. with 5. in 6. in 7. from; to 8. to 9. in 10. about

EXERCISE 8.2 Prepositions

1. Some parents don't make any effort to understand [**no preposition necessary**] teenagers. 2. **In** such situations, the workplace can provide a place for teens to interact with adult role models. 3. At work, teenagers can learn to form relationships **with** other people. 4. While they are in high school, students spend a lot of time **with** their friends or in class. 5. Work,

on the other hand, often requires teenagers to cooperate with people they may not know or like very well. **6.** Working also gives students something to do **in** (OR **during**) the hours after school. **7.** Teenagers with nothing to do after school are more likely to get **in** (OR **into**) trouble. **8.** A part-time job can allow teens to pay **for** leisure activities that they would otherwise be unable to afford. **9.** Having a little money to spend **on** things they want or need makes teenagers feel more independent. **10.** A teenager's ability to succeed both as a student and as a worker depends largely **on** his or her sense of responsibility.

EXERCISE 8.3 Prepositions

Frank Stoeber is responsible **for** one of the greatest roadside attractions **in** the state of Kansas. A farmer **by** trade, Frank would save pieces of string by rolling them **into** a ball. The more string that Frank would add, the larger the ball would grow. Instead of using the ball of string **for** other projects, Frank continued to add **to** it. When Frank donated the ball of string to the town **of** Cawker City, it was enormous. **Over** one and one half million feet of string was rolled **within** an 11-foot-wide ball. It was the largest ball of string in Kansas. To ward **off** any potential record breakers, Cawker City holds an annual Twine-A-Thon so that the famous ball of string started by Frank Stoeber can continue to grow.

EXERCISE 8.4 Prepositions

1. in **2.** to **3.** of **4.** up **5.** from **6.** down **7.** toward **8.** on **9.** under **10.** in OR within

EXERCISE 8.5 Idiomatic Verbs

1. up **2.** off **3.** out **4.** to **5.** up **6.** with **7.** into **8.** up with **9.** out **10.** down

EXERCISE 8.6 Idiomatic Verbs

1. out **2.** up **3.** into **4.** on **5.** out **6.** out **7.** up **8.** down **9.** over **10.** out

EXERCISE 8.7 Idiomatic Verbs

1. My idea was that kids who smoked cigarettes turned **out** to be the coolest kind in school. **2.** They came **out** with unusual things to say and they wore cool clothes. **3.** I admired them so much that I would go **along** with whatever they said we should think or do. **4.** One day I put **on** my coolest clothes and decided to try a cigarette, too. **5.** I looked **forward** to being more like them. **6.** But when I tried it, the cigarette tasted so disgusting that I wanted to throw up. **7.** I started to look at those kids in a new way, and I no longer wanted to take **after** them. **8.** They did not seem to notice that I did not want to hang **out** OR **around** with them anymore. **9.** I realized that I had put **up** with their silly ideas for a long time. **10.** From that day on, I decided to stick **with** friends who did not try so hard to be cool.